Trains, Boats and Jaunting Cars:

The holiday adventures of two Edwardian ladies

Edited by Nigel McBride

Published by

**MELROSE
BOOKS**

An Imprint of Melrose Press Limited
St Thomas Place, Ely
Cambridgeshire
CB7 4GG, UK
www.melrosebooks.co.uk

FIRST EDITION

Copyright © Nigel McBride 2017

The Editor asserts his moral right to
be identified as the owner of this work

Cover designed by Melrose Books

ISBN 978-1-912026-13-5
epub 978-1-912026-14-2
mobi 978-1-912026-15-9

Printed and bound in Great Britain by:
Ashford Colour Press Ltd
Unit 600
Fareham Reach
Fareham Road
Gosport
PO13 0FW

Contents

Foreword

These diaries belonged to Jane Mary Crisfield, my great-aunt. They were written by Jane and her friend, Eva Hitching, as an account of the various holidays they took together or with other friends between 1907 and 1938. They travelled extensively in the UK and Europe (notably France and Switzerland).

The original handwritten notebooks were found among family history papers handed down through the generations.

Jane Crisfield was born in 1882. She grew up in North London, the second of seven children, and was known affectionately throughout her life as 'Sis' to family and friends. She worked for a silversmith, James Deakin and Co. in Charterhouse Street, a stockbroker, and for many years for Harding, Tilton & Hartley – the company which imported Van Heusen shirt collars to the UK. Jane eventually became export manager and moved with the company from London to Taunton during WW2. After the war she retired and settled in Amersham, where she lived until her death in 1976.

Eva Hitching was also born in 1882, and grew up in the village of Finchingfield, Essex, the youngest of four sisters. She worked as a draper's clerk at Crisp and Co. in North London, and later worked at Bourne and Hollingsworth in Oxford Street. Eva married Charles Thomas in 1945, and also lived in Amersham. She died in 1955.

Some of the early holidays are marked 'Polytechnic'. The Polytechnic Touring Association was formed by the Regent Street

Polytechnic, and organised trips in Britain and overseas for its staff and students, also attracting customers from among non-Polytechnic members. The trips pioneered cheaper travel, making it accessible to less affluent travellers, and the Association became a substantial business, advertised in Bradshaw's Continental Railway Guide and elsewhere. In the 1960s it was taken over by the firm of Henry Lunn Ltd. to form the travel retailer Lunn Poly.

The diaries form a fascinating account of travel in the early 20th Century and illustrate the stamina required to undertake such journeys. Sadly, there was no photographic record of the trips, but photographs have been added to help to bring the text to life. Every effort has been made to attribute them correctly, and I would like to thank all those people who so kindly gave permission for their use.

Finally, I would like to thank my family for all their help and encouragement in developing and completing this project, especially for the original idea!

Nigel McBride
Stafford
April 2017

1.

August 1907
A week in Scotland (Polytechnic)

Saturday

12 o'clock left Kings Cross, arrived Edinburgh 10 o'clock after a most enjoyable and interesting journey and good company. The country was very flat until we passed York, Durham very pretty, the cathedral grand, standing very high, had a splendid view of it.

Newcastle very dirty and ugly little houses, river lovely. Berwick very pretty, got a good view of the sea.

As we crossed the Tweed, a hearty cheer went up for Scotland. From here we travelled all the way along the coast, the views were lovely, blue sea and rugged coast, the air seemed grand but rather fresh. It soon got dark, so that we were unable to see much of the coast as we came into Edinburgh. When we alighted from the train, several boys came rushing for our luggage, talking foreign language to us, and one man tried to embrace me. Anyway, we soon found our party and were on our way to Ramsay Lodge, after nearly falling over some drunken men.

Ramsay Lodge is a lovely old house. In the hall and up the staircase lots of Chinese lanterns were hanging, giving it a very pretty effect. We had supper in a large room with peculiar paintings and carvings on the walls, this is the University Hall. All up the staircase are interesting photos and carvings. Jean and I have a pretty little room to ourselves, for which we are very glad. We scribbled a few postcards then went for a short stroll, some funny old woman stopped us and jabbered away. At last we understood that she meant that it was not safe for us to go out alone, which scared us a bit. Jean imitated her in her talk but she did not seem to mind, and we had a real good laugh when she left us. On coming in, we explored the house and found a nice comfortable sitting room and lovely garden overlooking Princes Street, looks as if we get a grand view. Shall see better tomorrow.

Figure 1: *Ramsay Lodge and Ramsay Garden from Princes Street*

Sunday

Had a glorious day, continual sunshine. Went down to prayers and sang *Holy, Holy, Holy*. Mr Studd read 103 Psalm, it was most impressive. After breakfast went up to the Castle to see the soldiers, afterward to the service at St Giles Cathedral, it was rather droney, it is a beautiful building. After lunch had long walk to Arthur's Seat, passed John Knox' house on the way, White Horse Hotel built 1583, very picturesque, Holyrood Palace, etc. We had a long climb, 800ft, wind terrific, when we reached the top had a most grand view, beautifully clear, could see for miles. Coming down, we had great difficulty in walking. Arrived home dead tired, had dinner, then went to the service at College Hall in the evening, it was most enjoyable. Mr Studd spoke some beautiful words and Robert Kay, Scotchman, gave a funny address. Home to bed.

Figure 2: *John Knox House*

Monday

Have had a glorious day. Woke too late for prayers, after breakfast took train to Stirling, very pretty journey. The Ochil Mountains on our right and the Wallace Memorial very lovely. Visited Stirling Castle and church, had a beautiful view from the Castle, Grampian range in the distance and lovely hills all around. Lunched at The Golden Lion Hotel.

After lunch took train to Rumbling Bridge, had a walk of 1½ miles along the beautiful falls of Cauldron Linn. It was a grand sight, no words could express.

The morning had been wet, but the sun shone gloriously in the afternoon making everything look grand.

Took train back past Loch Leven and the Benarty Hills. A beautiful sight, the hills are covered with lovely trees. Home about 6, to dinner 7.45, musical evening and then to bed.

Figure 3: *The Golden Lion Hotel*

Figure 4: *Cauldron Linn*

Tuesday

Train to Craigendoran, then steamer up Loch Long and Loch Goil to Arrochar, a sweet little place surrounded by mountains.

CRAIGENDORAN STATION, HELENSBURGH.

Figure 5: *Craigendoran Station*

Figure 6: *Craigendoran Pier*

Lunch at the Arrochar Hotel, then a mile walk to Tarbet, sweetly pretty but very wet, then train to Ardlui. The scenery to Ardlui nearly took my breath away.

Then steamer down the length of Loch Lomond, scenery too grand for words. One side the sun was shining on the mountains, at the back black clouds making the hills look quite purple, the contrast was magnificent. Saw Ben Lomond then train from Balloch home. Dead tired, we were out 12 hours.

Wednesday

Took train to Callander, a beautiful little place, then coach to the Trossachs.

The scenery was grand and the weather splendid, best day we have had. We lunched at the Trossachs Hotel, had a climb up one side of the hills, and gathered heather. One almost feels one cannot speak, the hills and trees and everything is so lovely with the lakes beneath. We took coach back and then train home. After dinner, a tram ride round Edinburgh.

Figure 7: *Trossachs Hotel*

Thursday

Our free day, are very glad it is a very wet morning. Stayed in and wrote
letters then had some jolly games. At lunchtime the rain ceased and we
went out to get lunch. Found a very nice little place and did good justice
to our lunch, including some lovely Scotch butter and scones. After lunch
did some shopping, then saw a motor going to Forth Bridge so jumped
in. We had only gone a few yards when we saw one of our friends, who
also got in. We had a lovely ride. The afternoon turned out very fine, had
a good view of the Forth Bridge, it is very wonderful. Took coach back,
then had dinner, afterwards went to the New College to our concert,
it was splendidly arranged. At the close we sang *Auld Lang Syne*, all
joining hands. Everyone seemed just wound up and all went home. Had
a long talk to Sunday friends in the dining room then to bed.

Friday

Breakfast 7.30. At 8.35 we took train to Blair Atholl, then had a beautiful walk through the Killiecrankie Pass, to the falls of Tummell. The scenery appeared more grand, if it were possible. The Falls are wonderful, we sat up for some time watching the water, could hardly hear anyone speak for the noise it made. We then walked back to the station and took lunch in the train. We saw beautiful scenery to Perth, alighted at Dunkeld on the way home, and spent two hours visiting the Cathedral and city. There is not much to see except the Cathedral, which is very old and practically a ruin, it is one of the oldest in Scotland. The scenery all around is very grand, we just saw the Birnham Woods but did not have time to go into them. Train home, and after dinner some games and to bed.

Figure 8: *Falls of Tummell*

Figure 9: *Dunkeld Cathedral*

Saturday

Breakfast 7.30, our last. We had various speeches at the breakfast table, then made for the station, which was not at all pleasant after such a ripping week as we have had. A good many had gone on to Fort William the previous evening, and those who were going elsewhere came to see us off and say goodbye. We had a very pleasant journey and lunch in the train, arrived at Kings Cross 5.30 then journeyed on to Liverpool Street for Finchingfield. Thus ended one of the most delightful holidays one could wish to spend.

2.

August 1909
A week in Cornwall (Polytechnic)

Saturday, August 7th

Started from Paddington 12.30 by the Cornish Riviera Express, arrived at Penzance 5.30. On arrival at 'Mount Prospect', we were greeted with a warm welcome from Mr. & Mrs. Howard and a cup of tea. We were charmed with our bedroom, it is a lovely big room and magnificent sea view and St Michaels Mount. Dinner at 8 o'clock, exceedingly well served, we have a small table holding four. Went for a short walk after dinner. Do not think much of the town on the whole, but our house and garden is charming.

Sunday

Prayers and breakfast at 9 o'clock. Afterwards, a short walk and then to chapel, we had nice little service, a bit sleepy, met Mrs & Miss Latimer. Went for lovely walk after chapel, by the sea and sat on the beach. Do not think much of Penzance itself, it is very quaint and quiet. After lunch we had a delightful lazy time, wrote some cards and a letter to Maysie and home. Tea was served on the terrace, then Gertie and I had a long walk by the sea to Newlyn. It is another quaint little place, with no suggestion of a promenade, a truly rural seaside place as one could imagine things used to be hundreds of years ago, but certainly could not imagine such a place still in existence.

Supper at 8.30 then some hymns and to bed.

Figure 10: *Newlyn Harbour*

Monday

Breakfast 8.30, and 9.30 we started on our coach drive to St Ives. It was a glorious morning, had a delightful drive with plenty of fun. We alighted at Carbis Bay and had a long walk down the cliffs to the sea where a most charming sight met our eyes.

The sea was a perfect blue and the sand a lovely yellow. The contrast was beautiful. It is indeed one of the sweetest bays I have seen. Then on to St Ives by the cliffs, there is a lovely beach. We walked through some of the most quaint streets with tiny little houses, most awful places to live in.

After lunch, took coach along the north coast road to Gurnard's Head. It was a delightful sight across the moors. We alighted and walked through the cornfields to Gurnard's Head and climbed to the top as far as it was safe to.

We had a charming view of a most glorious coast, the sea was like a pond. What a sight it would be on a stormy day. One feels almost too full for words to think that some of us are privileged to see such sights as these. Then back to a most welcome tea at a farmhouse, splits and cream, etc. Coach back across England to Penzance, arrive 6.15. Dinner 7.00 then a lovely lazy time in the garden listening to the band. We have quite made friends with all the folks, they are very jolly. To bed at 10 o'clock.

Tuesday

After breakfast, took coach to Logan Rock. On the way we stopped at St Buryan and looked over the church. Then coach again to Penberth, from there a walk for 1½ miles through Penberth Cove, a delightful little spot. We saw some real Cornish fishermen.

Figure 11: *Penberth Cove*

Figure 12: *Logan Rock*

Then on to Logan Rock and climbed to the top. I sat in the giant's armchair, saw the Logan Lady, a large rock which moves. The Logan Rock is grand, it is one huge mass of rocks.

Then on to Porthcurno, past the school of wireless telegraphy where they have 9 cables for abroad.

Figure 13: *Porthcurno School of Wireless Telegraphy*

From here our coach met up again and took us on to Land's End, a delightful drive with the sea nearly all round us. The coast is simply grand just here. We climbed over the rocks and saw Dr. Sintax Rock, and then looked over to see the last stones in England.

On some rocks, in the distance about two miles, is the Longship Lighthouse. There are three men always there. Sometimes the weather is so bad that the lighthouse is not visible from land.

Mr. Hughes took us to see the caves but we were not able to go into them. How magnificent it all is. How we all nearly wept at 4 o'clock when it was our time to start back for home. We could see the sea on both sides and at the back, and even Mounts Bay in the distance. We drove back through Sennen and St Just on the left. In the distance we saw Chapel Carn where Wesley preached his first sermon, and saw the rock on which he sat when he wrote 'Here on a narrow neck of land 'twixt two unbounded seas'. We passed through Crows-an-wra on to St Buryan, then home and dinner on arrival, and then Gertie and I walked to Marazion and tried to get over to Mounts Bay but found the causeway almost covered so we had to be disappointed. Saw a glorious sunset then motored home. Some music and to bed.

Wednesday

Train at 10 o'clock to Truro. We had some real good fun on the way, ours is a very jolly party. Alighted at Truro and visited the Cathedral. It is quite new, built only 20 yrs. The architecture is very fine.

Figure 14: *Truro Cathedral*

Figure 15: *"On the Way to Calvary" in Truro Cathedral*

There is a lovely monument done by Tinworth, a poor boy whom Ruskin took an interest in. It represents 'On the Way to Calvary' and is done in terracotta clay. It is very beautiful.

Took boat down the River Fal to Falmouth. Very pretty but nothing special. At Falmouth Gertie and I left the party and went by ourselves down to the beach. I paddled, it was lovely and we had a delightful rest. It was too hot to walk much. Had tea in the gardens – a charming spot with beautiful flowers all round. Train at 5.20 to Penzance. After dinner, a walk with Elsie and Gertie round the town. Back at 10 o'clock.

Thursday

Coach at 8.30 to Lizard, 25 miles. Alighted at Helston, arrived at Lizard 12.15 – a baking day but lovely driving. We left the rest of the party and walked down to the lighthouse and on to Lizard. Found Kynance Cove too far off, so walked back to the village. Had tea 4 o'clock, took coach for home. Arrived 8.15 after a delightful day. After dinner sat in the garden and then to bed.

Friday

Spent the day in Penzance. Bathed and visited the church and park. Beautiful tropical flowers growing in the park. After lunch sat in the garden. In the evening a walk to Gulval – a sweet little place and church. After dinner a walk and to bed.

Saturday

10 o'clock train to Paddington. Had a good send-off. How terrible to leave it all, but how lovely to look back on. How thankful I feel for such a glorious time and such perfect weather all the week.

3.

August 1911
A fortnight in Ireland (Polytechnic)

Friday night and Saturday, August 11th/12th

Left Paddington 8.45pm. Had a splendid journey and plenty of fun. Arrived Fishguard 3.30am. Glorious crossing, very smooth and brilliant moonlight. I could not sleep at all, so kept myself warm walking up and down the deck. Everyone else asleep. Train from Rosslare 8.45am. Such funny carriages, very bare and dirty. We were glad of a good breakfast. Arrived at Mallow one hour late. Lost our connection, so did not arrive at Killarney until 12 o'clock.

Figure 16: *Cahernane*

We were met by our host and drove to 'Cahernane' in jaunting cars. It is a beautiful house, ¼ mile from the road, through an avenue of trees. Large staircase and hall. Lunch then to bed until 5 o'clock. Walked round the grounds, very extensive and wild. Dinner at 7 o'clock then a walk into Killarney. It is a funny town, all the people garbed in shawls. They almost cover their faces, their eyes and nose are the only parts visible. Back to bed 10 o'clock.

Sunday
Walk before breakfast in the garden, then to chapel, service 11.30am. They call it the Protestant church. Very good sermon, quite low church. Back to lunch. After lunch a walk to Earl of Kenmare's estate. The park is beautiful and gardens simply gorgeous.

Figure 17: *Killarney House, seat of the Earl of Kenmare*

The view from the house gives an extensive view of the lake and Innisfallen Island and a more beautiful spot could not be chosen. Queen Victoria is supposed to have advised the Earl to build on this spot and our present King George is thinking of taking it as a royal Irish residence (so rumour goes). Cromwell is supposed to have given this as a present to the Kenmare family. Back to tea, then sat in the garden until supper. Music and to bed.

Monday

Glorious day. After breakfast we started for our trip on the lakes. Took brake through Killarney to Gap of Dunloe, rather an ordinary drive. Arrived at the Gap, some took ponies. I did not venture but did the seven miles on foot. The Gap is a wild gorge, separating the Tomies Mountain from the MacGillycuddy Reeks.

Figure 18: *Gap of Dunloe*

The scenery is grand. At every turn there is some new variety of scenery. The hills rise to 3,400ft, romantic little bridges we cross here and there. It is a most solitary place, absolutely deserted. There are a few cottages, the noted Kate Kearney's and Patrick cottages.

We find that the inhabitants live here all the year round. What must it be like? But they tell us there is very little snow. We come to the Black Lake and Black Valley, a beautiful spot with the mountains rising around. The sun only shines in this valley three months of the year. It looked quite black, a gloomy spot. The echoes in the Gap are really wonderful. Sometimes a cannon is let off; and it repeats itself again and again. At the head of the Gap is Lord Brandon's Demesne.

We pass through here to the Upper Lake. Here we take lunch on the banks of the lake, which is very acceptable. The lakes are most tranquil, and who cannot be charmed with them? As we wind in and out through the shades, at some parts it is very narrow, only sufficient space for a small boat. We glide along in a most peaceful state. We seem to be the only people in existence in this gorgeous spot. One could not describe it. There is change at every turn. First we pass the Upper Lake with picturesque islands at various intervals. The Eagle's Nest, a beautiful peak, 1100ft. Soon the Old Weir Bridge comes in sight, then we shoot the rapids. After this the Meeting of the Waters, here the three lakes meet.

We pass to the Middle Lake, the Colleen Bawn Caves are curious and picturesque, then on to the Lower Lake.

Figure 19: *Colleen Bawn Caves*

It is studded with about thirty islands. The chief island is the Innisfallen. Scenery is of the most tranquil and serene. We pass to our landing stage and the bottom of the gardens then walk up to the house. Tea and a rest until dinner. Had a lovely day and perfect weather.

Tuesday

Short walk before breakfast. Tried to find the kitchen garden but failed. After breakfast started for our circular tour to Muckross Abbey and Dinis Island. Morning was delightful and the drive most exquisite. We paid a shilling toll to admit us to the Demesne. The grounds are very beautiful and extensive. We went over the abbey ruins, which are very fine, built 1446, called the Franciscan Monastery.

Figure 20: *Muckross Abbey*

There is a large private house owned by Mr. Vincent, a very rich man. We drove round the lake to Dinis Island. We are in the same direction as yesterday, only today we drive round the lake and yesterday we were on it. Dinis Island is very sweet, there is one house on it. We lunched here and walked round the island. Got a good view of the rapids. After lunch we drove round the middle lake, scenery simply grand and the bracken and ferns most gorgeous. The trees and all the foliage are naturally grown.

We crossed the Wishing Bridge where a wish is granted in 24 hours. We then came to the Kenmare Road on our way home passing Muckross Abbey Hotel. Also a platform erected for Kerry dancing. We find these are erected every 5 miles in County Kerry for dancing on Sunday evenings.

There is one great thing lacking in Ireland, there are practically no birds. We hear they are numerous in the winter, but in the summer they go to the woods, but we heard no singing in the woods. This, I think, accounts for the perfect stillness which I have never noticed anywhere else so much.

We have tea in the garden and before dinner a walk to the lake. After dinner to the lake again and watch the sunset until quite dark. I shall never forget that evening, the perfect stillness and the beauty of the mountains and lakes beyond description. We came back with some of the friends. They piloted us home through the warren and coves and then to bed after a lovely day.

Wednesday

Started at 10 o'clock for MacGillycuddy Reeks. We turned off by the Earl of Kenmare's estate not touching Killarney. Soon we reached the deer park. It is a beautiful drive through the grounds. We saw several deer. There is lovely bracken, ferns in profusion, and we soon reach the Robber's Glen and alight and walk through the glen to the Robber's Bridge. The Glen is a perfect mass of trees and ferns and some distance down there are rocks with running water. The bridge is almost covered with sweet little ferns. We join the brake again and drive to St. Finney, the oldest ruins in Ireland, built in the sixth century. The view here of the lower lake is grand, with the Mc Reeks, Tomies and Carrauntoohil rising in the distance (the highest mountain in Ireland), also Bucken Bridge, making a charming picture.

Figure 21: *MacGillycuddy's Reeks*

We drive on again to home and Western Park (Kenmare Estate). We lunch on the banks and plenty of fun, then rest on the bank of the lower lake. Tea at Mahony's cottage at Mahony's Point, then coach to Ross Castle and home very tired. We have our photos taken before dinner. After dinner we walk to Killarney to see the Kerry dancing. Home 11 o'clock.

Thursday

Short walk before breakfast. We leave our party and hire a jaunting car on our own. We had our photos taken, but unfortunately they were not a success. The reins came across my face. Drove into Killarney, looked over the St Franciscan Priory then on to the Seven Sisters. They are seven stones which have grown naturally and stand a great height above the ground.

It was a pretty drive, we were on the outskirts of the Deer Park, a road with a mass of trees on either side. We arrived back in the town at 2 o'clock and went into the Catholic cathedral. We were rather disappointed in it. Expected to see it more elaborate.

Walked around the town into the lace school, home to afternoon tea. Arranged a short programme for the evening after dinner. We all stayed in and had a very jolly time indeed. Music and dancing etc. We finished with Auld Lang Syne about 11.30pm.

Friday

Said goodbye to friends at Cahernane with a very heavy heart. Eight of us left at 10 o'clock by motor. About twenty friends came to see us off and gave us a hearty adieu. It was very sad to have to say goodbye. We had a glorious run, it was a perfect morning. We passed Muckross Demesne and Muckross Hotel. The road was like a switchback. We passed the Torc Cascade.

Figure 22: *Torc Cascade*

The wealth of foliage forms a marked contrast to the rugged mountains. We pass to the Long Range and get a good view of the Eagle's Nest and Purple Mountains. We reach the tunnel of the Kenmare road. On arrival at the top of the Upper Lake we alight and get a grand view of all the lakes. It was a sight one could never forget.

Further on we come to Windy Gap, and again alight to see the Kenmare Lake. We turn here on our way to Sneem and the scenery now is more barren. We are very high up. Sneem is quite a little village. Our next stop is at the Great Southern Hotel Parknasilla, a perfectly charming spot, absolutely ideal. The hotel is built in a most picturesque spot and the bay is lovely. The water looked a perfect blue and everything looked most tranquil and serene. We stayed here 1½ hours and left two friends who will come on to Glengarriff tomorrow. How I envy them.

We start again at 2.30pm. The scenery is not quite so grand from here to Kenmare. We journey along by the Blackwater river which is most lovely, and our road is sheltered on either side by a mass of trees which makes it very cool and pleasant. We alight to see a very pretty waterfall at the Blackwater Bridge. We arrive at the Great S Hotel Kenmare at 4 o'clock and start again at 4.30pm for Glengarriff.

Kenmare is very dirty but the hotel is very nicely situated. We soon reach the suspension bridge, where we all have to walk as it is not safe. We get most gorgeous views as we gradually ascend to the Caher Mountains. The road winds round and round in a most wonderful way. We rise to 600ft, there are 365 lakes in these mountains.

Near the summit we pass through a series of tunnels by which the road penetrates the mountains. We pass four, one of which is very long. On emerging into daylight, we get a grand view of the Caher Mountains, we are now in County Cork. In about six miles we reach Glengarriff. The road is very dangerous and there seems to be nothing but a tiny ledge between us and the huge valley beneath. It is all downhill and a very winding road. Anyway, we arrive quite safely. Glengarriff is in quite a valley and before reaching the village we pass through a beautiful avenue of trees. We have tea and a short walk and to bed.

Figure 23: *Tunnel near Glengarriff*

Saturday

There is a charming pool at the bottom of our garden called Poul Na Guron. There are lovely pine trees which give it quite an alpine style. We sit in our boat all the morning and write letters and postcards. In the afternoon walk to Roches Hotel to tea. This hotel is situated in one of the loveliest spots one could imagine. The view is grand with the mountains rising above the water.

We walked round the grounds and thoroughly enjoyed it. We are most charmed with Glengarriff. Language utterly fails to give even a limited idea of its beauty. It is a deep alpine valley, enclosed by rugged hills. The bay is supposed to contain thirty-four islands and these are covered with lovely foliage and ferns. It is a most serene spot, just a fit place to loll away the time and dream. One has no inclination to read, but simply to look on the beauties around. The view on the little pier is very sweet. Mountains rise one above the other in a most rugged fashion. If only this place were in England, what a world's wonder it would be. Instead, it is practically unknown. Tourists staying here imagine they can see it in a few hours, but it is impossible. At every turn there are fresh beauties, its great charm is the perfect tranquillity and soft seclusion.

Sunday

To church at 11 o'clock, very nice service. Afterwards a walk. On our way home we met Mr and Mrs Wean. In the afternoon explored Poul Na Guron and did some writing. Found another lovely spot at the end of the pool. Church in the evening, afterwards watched a most gorgeous sunset. The colouring varied every few moments and one only realises the beauties of Glengarriff as we see more of it. There is such an alpine style about it. A little music and to bed.

Monday

Boat at 10.30am to Bantry. Called at the Eccles to see Mr and Mrs Wean. We had a nice sail over to Bantry, but too short. We were absolutely disgusted with the place. It happened to be fair day, which made it heaps worse. There were cattle of all descriptions in the main street and the scent was dreadful. The houses are filthy and also the people. Not a clean spot to be found anywhere.

It was a scorching day and we got back as quickly as possible after seeing the town and sat on the cliffs. The bay is perfect, and we thoroughly enjoyed that part of it. We had 2½ hours to wait for the next boat and nothing to eat but blackberries. We could not fancy any hotel here. Went up to Roches after we got back and had a lovely tea. Arrived home 8 o'clock. We were amusing ourselves with music when Mr and Mrs Wean called. Had a very jolly evening with them, the drawing room to ourselves. They left at 11 o'clock after inviting us to spend the next day with them.

Figure 24: *Bantry Fair Day*

Tuesday

Met Mr and Mrs Wean at 10 o'clock and took a small boat all round the bay. Landed to see the waterfall, climbed all amongst the rocks, got a good view of the castle. The islands are lovely, there are thirty-four, and we had a delightful and interesting time rowing in and out amongst them. A seal followed us a little distance. We gradually made our way to Poul Na Guron. The pool looks even more lovely from the water. By waiting a little time for the tide, we were able to get up to Cromwell's Bridge (supposed to have been built in twenty-four hours).

Figure 25: *Cromwell's Bridge, Glengarriff*

It is a sweet spot. There is only just room for a small boat to pass, and the trees hanging into the water and little ferns everywhere. We got back again into the bay and passed by Garnish Island (bought by Mr Brice, an American). The coast everywhere is lovely, very rugged. We got a grand view from the water, landed about 2 o'clock, spent the rest of the time eating blackberries. Left our friends at 5 o'clock after a very happy day. After tea a short walk on the Castletown Road, but it was too weird to go far. Then home to bed.

Wednesday

Said goodbye to our friends at 10.30 then spent the morning on the hill back of the Eccles. We had a lovely view of the bay and island. Lunch at Roches Hotel and a lazy afternoon on the hills. Home to tea, music in the evening.

Figure 26: *Jaunting car*

Thursday

Our last day at Glengarriff. Hired a jaunting car and went for a lovely drive on the Castletown Road. Most lovely scenery, quite equal to anything we have yet seen, better if anything. We drove all along by the sea, the mountains are very rugged this side. We went up a tremendous height and were quite close to the Sugarloaf Mountain. There was a house here and there but everywhere seemed quite deserted. The sea gave it a charming sight and we saw Bear Island in the distance. We were about thirteen miles from Castletown. Came back the same road, arriving 1 o'clock. Blackberrying in the afternoon. Tea at Eccles Hotel and a walk in the evening, then home to pack.

Friday

Left Poul Na Guron 10 o'clock. Caught the 10.30 motor to Bantry. It was a very pretty run with a fine view of Bantry Bay. Train to Cork from the Cork Bandon and South Coast Railway. We proceeded to the Great Southern and Western Railway and left our luggage. Took tram to St Patrick's Street. Lunch at Thompson's. After lunch went into Peter and Paul's Church just round the corner.

Very fine buildings and decorations, rather elaborate. From here to the Court House and on to the Protestant Cathedral. A beautiful building and very nice inside. Walked from here to the university through Fitzgerald Park. Very pretty indeed, very like our London parks but the town is very ordinary, although in the distance it is exceedingly pretty. Cork is built on a hill, the houses rise one above the other with the river beneath. We arrived back at St Patrick's Street and found we had time to go to Black Rock, so took a car there and back. The river is very pretty at Black Rock, it is just a suburb of Cork. Tea at Thompson's then made our way to the station, caught the Fishguard express at 7.40. Met some Poly friends at Mallow.

Very good crossing, fairly smooth, could not sleep so walked up and down the deck and enjoyed the sea breezes. It seemed very weird to be on the open sea in the middle of the night. Very interesting to watch the flashlights. Breakfast on the train at 6 o'clock. Arrived Paddington 10.05am, one hour late, feeling not at all pleased to leave the lovely country and scenery and to be back to the ordinary routine after such a varied and enjoyable fortnight. Still all good things must end.

4.

August 1912
Ten days in Wales – Pwllheli

Friday night, August 23rd

Left Euston 8 o'clock. Very good train. Had a comfortable journey, carriage to ourselves and arrived at Pwllheli 7 o'clock. Had a nice journey and interesting from Holywell. The sea looked grand. Was very interested in the Menai Bridge which separates Carnarvonshire from Anglesey. Had a good view of Llandudno, Colwyn Bay and Carnarvon Castle etc. The weather was lovely to greet us and we walked to the South Beach Hotel. It is in a fine position quite on the seafront.

Figure 27: *Gimblet Rock*

Have a good view of the Gimblet Rock, lovely view of the Rivals and Snowdon. Also the St Tudwal Islands. We were too early for breakfast so had a blow by the sea. After breakfast walked on the beach to Gimblet Rock and did our first bit of climbing, so sat down for some time and then had a good look round the town. The town is about ten minutes' walk from the seafront. It is very old-fashioned and the trams are most quaint, like a luggage trolley with forms on.

Figure 28: *Pwllheli tram*

After lunch a rest by the sea. We like the hotel very much. Everything promises a good time. Pwllheli has a background of mountains, Snowdon and Cader Idris on the left. The beach is four miles long and a lovely expanse of open sea. There are such a lot of chapels in the town and are called by a certain name such as 'Sedrow' and 'Baalam'. Cannot find the reason for this. After tea we took a pretty walk to Pen-y-Garron or 'Gayn', down Ala Road, then a footpath and climbed to the top. The view ascending was lovely and at the top a gorgeous sight for miles around. We could see fields upon fields and a background of mountains and sea in the front. It was well worth the stiff climb. We descended down Salem Hill. Dinner 7 o'clock. After dinner a blow by the sea and to bed 9 o'clock, very early.

Sunday

After breakfast went to a service at 10 o'clock, in Welsh. Could not understand a word. Had a nice walk on the Abererch Road. Turned to the left after walking some distance and went to the back of the hill and climbed to the top. The air was lovely and we thoroughly enjoyed the blow. After lunch sat by the sea. In the evening went to the Presby Chapel and had a very nice service. Afterwards I went to an organ recital at the church. After supper a lovely moonlight walk on the beach to the Gimblet Rock. It was a walk I shall never forget. Did not want to leave the sea, it looked so inviting.

Monday

Very wet morning. Our day for Beddgellert. We took coach at 9.30 on the Abererch Road. We passed through Afon Wen, a small village, then on to Llanystumdwy where Lloyd George was brought up. There is a nice library being built by him for the inhabitants. From here the scenery gets very pretty. We soon come to Criccieth, a very charming spot. A nice house where Lloyd George lives. It was very wet so we did not stay. We soon come to Tremadoc and Portmadoc. Scenery very lovely, huge mountains covered with lovely heather and bracken and the River Aberglaslyn beneath. Here and there are lovely little waterfalls. We soon come to the Pass of Aberglaslyn. From here to Beddgellert the scenery could not be surpassed. The fir trees give it quite an alpine appearance, growing up the mountains which appear to reach the cloud. We lunched at Saracen's Head Hotel.

After lunch take a walk to see the falls then coach back at 3 o'clock. The village of Beddgellert stands at the junction of three vales, Glaslyn and Colwyn. A noted feature is the tomb of Gellert, Llewellyn's faithful dog, just on the outskirts of the village. The name is supposed to have been taken from him.

We alighted at Criccieth on our way back, and had a lovely walk up to the castle. The view at the top amply repaid us for the stiff climb. We could see for miles around. Arrived home about 6.45. After dinner a walk by the sea.

Tuesday

Up very early. Walked over to Gimblet Rock, had a nice blow. Glorious morning. Did some writing and climbing. After breakfast, four of us took tram from West Beach to Llanbedrog, a very enjoyable ride all along by the sea in the funny little trams. We went over Glyn-y-Weddw Hall, a lovely mansion now open to the public (6d entrance). There is a fine collection of pictures.

Figure 29: *Glyn-y-Weddw Hall*

The view obtained from the house is most lovely. The grounds cover 50 acres and are beautifully laid out with lovely flowers. We climbed up very high through a warren and got over the wall and climbed to the top of the Llan hills, 433ft. We obtained a fine view of Abersoch and the sea beyond the peninsula. We lost Mr Lea and found him, after an hour's search, down below outside the gardens. After lunch, coach to Nefyn through the Boduan Woods. The woods are very lovely.

Nefyn is a sweet spot, an ideal place for a quiet holiday, but away from everywhere. It has a huge bay and the sands are very hard and quite yellow. The cliffs rise to a very great height and surround the bay. We got some nice views, had a nice long time to look around. All thoroughly enjoyed ourselves, it was a very happy afternoon. Five of us found a nice little cottage for tea then immediately had to take the coach home. After dinner, a long walk in the moonlight on the sand, other side of the town.

Wednesday

Tram to Llanbedrog and a walk of three miles to Abersoch, a simple little watering place. We got a good view of St Tudwal's Island. Motor back to lunch. Afternoon coach to Nanhoron Valley, on our way we passed Llanengan. We ascend a lovely hill, where we get a magnificent view and very extensive. We soon come to the valley and one fails to find words to express it. There are hills rising to a great height on either side, covered with a mass of trees. We alight at a little cottage and roam about for about a half hour, then coach back.

Near Abersoch the scenery was even more lovely, and we passed a very high hill with a little turret, which is quite a landmark of ours in Pwllheli. Had a lovely view on the top of this hill of Pwllheli Bay and Gimblet Rock. We then came to Llanbedrog down a terrible hill. Home 6 o'clock. Sea glorious, so had a good blow for half an hour before dressing for dinner. After dinner a short walk. Very heavy sea, we got nearly drenched with the spray. Too rough to be out.

Thursday

A blow before breakfast. Sea very rough but a lovely day. Train at 9.50 for Betws-y-Coed, Cambrian Railway to Minffordd Junction. On our way had a good view of Criccieth. Changed to the Ffestiniog Toy Railway for Blaenau Ffestiniog. These trains are most quaint, more like a tram and very tiny. We sat in a carriage lengthways.

The scenery to Blaenau Ffestiniog is grand, about 13 miles. We gradually rise until in one place we are 700ft above Portmadoc. The curves are so sharp that it is possible to see both ends of the train. We could see Harlech Castle on the right and after Penrhyn Station we get a most charming view of Dwyryd Valley. Beautiful hills and trees rising in all directions and houses appearing here and there amongst the trees.

We come to Tan-y-Bwlch, a lovely spot, it means 'under the pass'. Maentwrog is our next station. Here and there on our journey we pass lovely little waterfalls. We pass Ddualt and next to that Tanygrisiau (under the steps). Then we come to Blaenau Ffestiniog Junction.

There we take the L&NW Railway to Betws. We get a good view of the Palmerston quarries. The slate looks just like coal and rises to a great height. A sight I was very interested to see. There are little railways running here and there up the mountains to convey the coal. Ffestiniog looks to be a good sized place. We get some more charming scenery from here to Betws. Beautiful vales and hills covered with heather and gorse. It all made an impression I shall never forget and shall often long to take that train journey from Pwllheli to Betws.

There are some charming houses some distance from Betws and a lovely river rushing along called Glyn Lledr. We pass Roman Bridge Station and Dolwydellan and on to Betws. We make our way to the Miners' Bridge.

Figure 30: *Miners' Bridge, Betws-y-Coed*

The village we pass on our way is small and built in a valley with mountains rising all round. The Miners' Bridge is sloping. We walked over and watched the water rushing along on the other side.

Then another walk of 1¼ miles to the Swallow Falls, which are considered the finest in Wales, and they are indeed very fine. We clambered to the bottom but got very wet with the spray so had to come away and watch them from the top. Back to the village for lunch. In the afternoon walked to the Fairy Glen, very pretty walk. We sat for some time in the glen on the rocks and watched the water rushing over, dreaming all the time. Had a cosy, jolly little tea, which we badly wanted. Then caught the 6.40 train home, arrived Pwllheli 10pm very tired but very full up with all the glorious things we had seen.

Friday

A blow by the sea before breakfast. At 11 o'clock took coach for the Rival Mts. We took the Carnarvon road, had a good view of the bay but on the whole the drive was rather ordinary. We were within about 11 miles of Carnarvon, it is a very good road. We passed the Three

Crosses, a small village and alighted at Llanaelhaearn. Here we take the road opposite the little inn for its ascent of Tre'r Caeiri, the most important of the Rivals, 1887ft. The panorama of sea and mountains is remarkable and we had a remarkably clear day, not a cloud to be seen and brilliant sunshine. On one side Pwllheli and Criccieth etc. and on the other Carnarvon and Anglesey and Nefyn. We sat down several times and enjoyed the scenery and had our sandwiches, then went back and had a cosy tea at the village inn. The rest of the time we spent on the hills roaming round. Coach back 5.15, arriving home at 6.45. After dinner a moonlight walk and to bed.

Saturday

Very tired, did not get up early. Saw Mr B. off by the 9.50 train. Lovely morning then a walk round the town, afterwards sat on Gimblet Rock. Sea very calm. After lunch tram to Llanbedrog and climbed on the hill. Spent the afternoon there, back to dinner and a short stroll after.

Sunday

Service morning at Cong chapel and a walk along West Beach. Very lively there. In the afternoon climbed Pen-y-Garn and the evening I spent by myself on the Gimblet Rock.

Monday

My last blow at 7 o'clock and caught the 7.55 train for home. Was sorry to leave it. We had a very pleasant journey, very pretty and interesting. The sea looked so very inviting. It was sad to have to leave it all. Arrived Euston 4.30.

5.

July 1913
Two weeks' tour in Switzerland

Friday/Saturday July 18th/19th

Left Victoria at 8.45pm. Had a splendid send-off. Arrived Dover 10.30. Very calm crossing, not at all cold. Arrived Ostend 3am. It looks a very nice place, but scarcely light enough to tell. Train for Basle, we pass through Bruges. It is just like one would imagine, peculiar little buildings and houses, seems rather smoky. Passed the Ghent Exhibition. After passing Brussels had a very welcome *café complet* breakfast. The scenery is very ordinary all the way. The people look very strange, full of working men, women going to market. The women with no hats and carrying huge baskets. Short stay at Luxembourg, very dirty station. No pretence at smartness. Metz, a large city, looks rather nice. Arrive at Basle 4.30 and a nice tea waiting for us.

Two hours in Basle, so took the tram down to the Rhine. The town is very picturesque, such pretty houses, very quaint. It all seems very novel. At 6.30 train for Lucerne. The scenery soon starts to be very fine and glorious hills and valleys with lovely trees and sweet little chalets here and there, covered with lovely flowers. We arrive at Lucerne 9.15pm. A grand reception awaiting us, rockets and fireworks on the lake and the hotel beautifully illuminated and coloured lights burning in the gardens giving them all a lovely colour. We cross the lake and arrive at the chalet and a warm welcome awaits us. Garden illuminated, a supper then to bed.

Sunday

Very wet morning and not much of a view of the mountains. It is a charming place, and on our way to church, crossing the lake, the rain ceased. The sun gave everything a grand look. After church, joined some friends and walked back along the lake.

Figure 31: *Hotel National, Lucerne*

The hotels are most charming and the grounds of the National are lovely, glorious flowers growing in profusion. The chalets also are just lovely and extend right down to the lake edge. The pictures too, are beautiful, various scenes in Switzerland. My room overlooks the lake and I get a charming view of Pilatus and the Burgenstock range and the peaceful, tranquil lake beneath and mountains rising all around. In the afternoon, a walk in the woods, and got some grand views.

Service in the evening. After, a stroll until 10.30 in the courtyard illuminated. Very clear night, could see the lights on Pilatus and Stanserhorn and the searchlight over the lake.

Monday

Figure 32: *Rigi Mountain Railway and Lake Lucerne*

Got our first view of Pilatus at 6am. Sun shining gloriously, a perfect sight. Walk by the lake before prayers. Boat across the lake to Vitznau, a sweet little village then mountain railway to Rigi. On the way we get lovely views of the lake and mountains everywhere, a continual train of romantic beauty. Mountains covered in magnificent trees. On the top, 5905, we get a grand view, quite impossible to put into words.

I stood for 15 minutes entranced at a landscape of more than 200 mountains and 14 lakes. Villages, towns and meadows lie at our feet. One's heart goes out in thankfulness to the Giver of these grand things. Every few minutes the scene varies in colour, one minute a cloud covers the mountain, then the next it is bathed in sunshine. After lunch we walked part of the way down. We saw some fine St Bernard dogs, visited the little pilgrims' chapel built in a rock used for the shepherds.

Tea at the Kaltbad Hotel, a magnificent place where one could just dream the time away and live it over again when business life comes crowding in all sorts of things. It is said to be the loveliest spot on the Rigi. We then take train down to Vitznau and home, not tired but full up with seeing so much. After dinner a walk into Lucerne and a look round the town. It is most brilliant and very interesting, quaint buildings. Home by the 10.30 boat, just glorious on the lake.

Tuesday

Sat by the lake, writing until 11am. Explored the walks at the back of the chalet. At 12.00 boat for Pilatus. Charming morning, lovely sail. Put in at several pretty little places. Met the friends at Stansstad who had spent the night on the Stanserhorn. Arrived at the Alpnachstad and took mountain railway to the summit.

Figure 33: *Pilatus railway*

The scenery grand, Lucerne Lake lying at an enormous depth. We pass through four tunnels, the ascent is exceedingly steep. On reaching the top, a glorious sight met our view – Lake Lucerne and the Oberland meadows and woods. A most grand sight. We climbed to the top of Esel, 6962, and got an even more extensive view, snow-capped mountains, a sight never to be forgotten. We walked around through tunnels cut in the rock and started walking down. On our way back had some snowballing and enjoyed the walk immensely. It was very steep and rough walking. Took train halfway, would not care to walk it all. Lovely sail on the lake home, on the way had a thunderstorm which gave a grand finish-up. Wet evening, stayed in and had music.

Wednesday

Very wet. After breakfast decided to venture and take the Engelberg extra excursion. Steamer to Stansstad then electric train. Our next important station is Stans, the capital of Nidwalden. We passed by the foot of the Stanserhorn, with the Buchserhorn on our left, the beautiful valleys of Engelberg beneath. We soon reach Dallenwil. Here and there we pass crucifixes and the scenery gets very charming. Our view to a great extent is hidden by the clouds. At the electric power station, an engine is put on the back to take us up the mountain to Engelberg. It is a grand sight.

We pass through beautiful pinewoods and the water rushing beneath. As we rise higher and higher, we get views of the snow mountains. Engelberg is a great centre for winter sports, a charming spot surrounded by huge mountains. We seem to be in quite a different part of Switzerland. The people appear to be much more countrified and isolated. Have never seen so many crucifixes erected anywhere else, every few yards we pass one. The houses look very old and most picturesque and the church is simply wonderful, one mass of gorgeous paintings, elaborate to the extreme.

We walk to the Teufelsbrucken Falls in the pouring rain, but quite enjoyed it, but one does not see the best under such aspects. The mountains are lovely, Titlis, 10626, rising above us. Engelberg itself is 4000ft high. We take train again at 4 o'clock. Rather cold on the boat, so we played games on the deck to keep us warm and have a very jolly time. In the evening we have a reunion, dancing and music, which was exceedingly jolly. Afterwards a gossip in the courtyard, impossible to think of keeping early hours here. At every turn there is some new excitement. To bed 11.45.

Thursday

Wet in the morning but proved to be a very fine day. Lovely trip down the lake to Flüelen (Lake of the 4 Cantons), on our way passing Tell's Chapel.

Figure 34: *William Tell's Chapel*

Picturesque landscapes rise before our eyes. We wind in and out and every way we turn a magnificent view is before us, the mountains covered in glorious green, and flowers and trees of all descriptions. Rigi on our left and Pilatus on our right. We soon come to the Axenstrasse with its galleries excavated in the rock and the Bristenstock towering above us.

At Flüelen (a sweet little village at the end of the lake) we take the train to Göschenen. We get a glimpse of the St Gotthard tunnel. This is a grand trip up the valley of the Reuss with the river rushing beneath. We gradually rise higher and higher. A church is seen in three different positions. After passing through many tunnels we rise to a good height and get magnificent views of lovely valley and majestic mountains and gorges. What a grand sight it all is, one we can never forget. On reaching Göschenen we alight and have a very still climb of 3½ miles through the Schollenen Pass to the village of Andermatt. It is well worth the exertion.

On our way we passed the Devil's Bridge, where the Reuss here forms a fine waterfall. We are now 5000ft high. We are for some time held up by the blasting. On reaching Andermatt we have lunch at the Great Central Hotel then a visit to the church, which is very elaborate, and a walk round. Have a splendid lecture from Mr. Mitchell on the history of Andermatt. Here we are, close to the Grimsel Pass and the route which is taken for Rhone glacier, fairly near the borders of Italy.

Train home, some good fun on the way. On the boat, meet 300 Austrians. We join with them in alternately singing popular airs and so have a very pleasant journey home. A good ending to a lovely trip. After dinner, take the motor boat into Lucerne to visit the casino. It is very brilliant. We watched the tables a little time and then sat and listened to the orchestra. Back by 11pm boat, got locked out. And so ended one of the most exciting days and full of enjoyment that one could imagine.

Friday

A glorious day. Boat into Lucerne at 10 o'clock. Walk around the town visiting the various places of interest. Walked over the famous bridge Kapellbrucke, which is very novel, mentioned in Longfellow's *Golden Legend* where there is also a mention of the pictures painted on the walls.

Figure 35: *Kapellbrucke, Lucerne*

Figure 36: *Lion Monument, Lucerne*

The town has some very old buildings. The various courts very much appeal to me and the old town hall is most picturesque. Organ recital in the cathedral at 12 o'clock, lunch at the Union Hotel. Afterwards a visit to the Glacier Gardens and the famous Lion of Lucerne, which is carved in a solid stone wall.

Went up the watchtower around the gardens, visited the War Museum, afterwards shopping and sat by the lake – most gloriously clear. The view of Rigi and Pilatus absolutely perfect. 5 o'clock boat back, then a ramble in the woods at the back of the chalet before dinner. After dinner said farewell to the friends leaving. Saw them off by the boat, it was sad to see so many go after such a happy week. How glad I am it is my privilege to have another week.

A most perfect sunset. Walked by the lake and watched it for about an hour, everywhere bathed in scarlet and the Engelberg range in the distance with a beautiful glow on the snow. 9 o'clock it vanished gradually, the lights of Lucerne appear.

Saturday

Glorious morning, Pilatus perfectly clear. Could see the hotel on it quite clearly. A large number of friends came over to the station to see us off. Great cheering from Seeburg. Caught the 9.30 train for Meiringen. We pass by the side of Pilatus to Alpnachstadt, lovely scenery. We soon come to Sarnen Valley and the lake of Sarnen.

Here we get a grand view, mountains rising all round and the beautiful valley beneath. The lake is 5 miles long and we travel quite on the edge of it. Everyone leaves the carriage deserted and we all take our place on the platform. We pass Lake Lungern and through wonderful scenery to the Brunig Pass.

On reaching Brunig we alight for 25 minutes. We resume our journey and descend to the valley of Meiringen. We are a great height and get a splendid view of the valley. It appears very flat and gives a charm to the mountains.

Figure 37: *Hotel du Sauvage, Meiringen*

We alight at Meiringen and go to Sauvage Hotel. A charming place, beautiful flowers in profusion and a fountain playing. From my room I get a grand view of the mountains and the Alpbach gorge. A charming place to stay at.

Figure 38: *Gorge of the Aare*

After lunch walk to the Gorge of the Aare, a wonderful place. There are platforms built on one side so that it is possible to walk right through the gorge. Just got back in time to avoid a soaking by the thunderstorm. Dinner splendidly served, the Alpbach Falls very prettily illuminated.

Sunday

Lovely day. Went to church. I played and another tolled the bell, and six others made the choir. A short stroll round the village, visiting the church. After lunch a delightful wander through the woods to the Alpbach Falls. Get gorgeous views of the valley and mountains. It is ideal. From the hotel had a grand view through the telescope of the Wellhorn and could see the snow lying very thick. In fact, could have recognised a person, it was so clear. This is a very peaceful spot, no sound to be heard but the rushing of the gorges. Just an ideal spot to spend a Sunday in. Church in the evening. After dinner a short stroll and some music.

Monday

With much regret, we pack up and leave this delightful spot. We all want to stay longer. Extremely hot, sun shining gloriously. Take train to Brienz, then on the lake to the Giessbach Falls.

Figure 39: *Giessbach Funicular and Falls*

Take the funicular railway up to the hotel. We climbed up through the woods and got great views of the falls. It is in six distinct parts. In one place we were able to walk right under it. It was delightfully cool. We stood for some long time enjoying the cool and delicious spray, saw a rainbow in the spray. Lunch at the Giessbach Hotel. Sat outside and so enjoyed the view of the gorge and the beautiful fir trees and the lake a most beautiful blue. Quite the prettiest we have had. Boat to Interlaken down the Brienz Lake. Some friends unfortunately leave us to go to Grindelwald.

Our Hotel Des Alps is in the Hoheweg. There is a lovely entrance hall and piano and the gardens are very charming. It is quite a large town and the River Aare runs through it from the Brienz Lake to the Thunersee. Here we get a grand view of the Jungfrau, 12400. We made the acquaintance of a Russian professor and spent an enjoyable hour listening to his playing. After dinner to the Kursaal.

Figure 40: *Kursaal, Interlaken*

It is supposed to be the finest in Switzerland. There is a grand orchestra of fifty and they played some of Wagner's music. The people sit about most gaily dressed and very smart. We sat for some time eating ices and enjoying the music, watched the table, then a stroll round the grounds which are very delightful.

Tuesday

Walk through the town to Heimvehfluh, it is a fairly stiff climb through woods. Had a lovely view from the top of the valley. Interlaken takes its name from the fact that at one time Thunersee and Brienz were one lake, now divided by the town of Interlaken. After lunch, a delightful rest in the garden.

It is very hot here. Later went for a delightful ramble through the town. Came to Unspunnen, found ourselves eventually on the way to Heimvehfluh, a very delightful walk and one thoroughly enjoyed. Had tea in one of the sweetest of gardens, Swiss pastries under a Japanese umbrella, all very romantic. After dinner sat in the garden and had some good fun.

Wednesday

Train at 9.30 through the Lauterbrunnen valley, a most perfect day, sky cloudless. It is a sweet valley and I think the scenery impressed me more than any I have yet seen. Water rushing beneath and the mountains rising, covered in glorious trees and everything looking such a perfect colour. On reaching Lauterbrunnen we change for the mountain railway. On our way we see the Falls of Trummelbach and above are the Jungfrau, the Eiger 3975 and Monch 4000. Screams of delight as we gradually get higher and higher and nearer the snow mountains. We reach the Scheidegg Kleine 7000 and here alight.

Figure 41: *Kleine Scheidegg*

A good many of us climb another 1000ft and go through the ice grotto and are able to actually climb onto the snow. Our boots get soaked, as the heat is melting the snow so quickly. But they soon dry, as the ground is burning with the heat of the sun. The light seems very strong and almost seems too much. After lunch take train down to the valley of Grindelwald, stay at the Adler, a lovely spot, beautiful gardens. The Schreckhorn (over 12,000ft) just opposite and the Wetterhorn (over 13,000) on our left. Wet evening, stayed in and had games.

Thursday

Started at 9 o'clock for our long climb to the glacier. Twenty-three of us in all, only seven ladies ventured. It was a very stiff climb for 2 hours with short rests in between.

Figure 42: *Baregg Glacier*

At the hut we had lunch and a rest for an hour then a very rough climb to the Baregg glacier. We had great fun being roped together but soon found it was very necessary, as in some parts it was very dangerous. It was a delightful experience, the glacier was a delightful blue, and huge openings with the water rushing. The guide had to cut places for our feet and we all landed the other side after 1½ hours quite safely.

In the distance we heard loud noises like thunder and found it was snow falling. We had a lovely view of the snow mountains and they still seemed to be tremendously high, far above us, although we were 7,000ft. We sat down and had our photos taken and a good rest. Coming back we found some glorious flowers, beautiful forget-me-nots an abundance of varieties, never seen such charming wild flowers. We strolled home at our own free will, visited the ice grotto and only arrived just in time for dinner, the last of the party. Tea in the garden. After dinner a long walk round the town, lovely glow on the mountains, and then sat in the garden until 11 o'clock. A most delightful day and one I shall never forget.

Friday

With a very heavy heart, I realise it is my last day in Switzerland. How I do long to stay longer. The garden looked just charming as I had a stroll before breakfast to take my last look on the beauties of the mountains. Everything bathed in sunshine, one literally had to tear oneself away from it. Train to Bern, it is a very pretty town and the River Aar very charming.

Visited the parliament buildings and saw the old noted clocktower and cathedral and the bear pits. Tea and then train to Basle, plenty of fun on the way. A glorious evening, making us feel very sad as we gradually leave Switzerland and arrive at Basle. After booking our luggage, we stroll round the town and see the old market place. Train at 11.40pm for Brussels, very comfortable journey. Alight at Brussels 8.30am.

Saturday

After breakfast at the Hotel du Nord go to bed for a few hours. In the afternoon take the train up the Boulevard des Alps, a beautiful street with trees on either side. See the Royal Palace and go into the park and then the Botanical Gardens. After dinner a short walk and to bed.

Sunday

Saw the *Palace des Justices* Museum and several churches. In the afternoon, Notre Dame and the St Marie Church, the noted archway which was erected to celebrate the independence of Brussels. After dinner sat on the balcony. It is a very noisy city and does not appeal after the beauties and peacefulness of Switzerland. It is strange to see the people sitting outside the restaurants and hotels drinking.

Monday

Train at 8.40 for Ostend. Very calm crossing to Dover, arriving Charing Cross 7 o'clock. So ends a delightful and never to be forgotten trip.

6.

August/September 1914
Three weeks' holiday in North and South Devon

Saturday August 29th

Figure 43: *Lynton and Barnstaple Railway*

Sis and I left Waterloo at 11 o'clock on Saturday morning, Aug 29th. We had a very pleasant journey, arriving at Barnstaple 4 o'clock, just in time to get some tea. Saw a wee bit of the town, it looks to be very quaint. At 5 o'clock we took the toy railway to Lynton. The gauge is only 2ft and the little carriages are very funny. We travel up the valley of the Yeo between hills gradually rising in height as we proceed, the valleys are charming and the hills purple and yellow with the heather and gorse. The rail winds round and round, and after travelling some distance we are yet only just the other side of the valley. We pass tiny little stations, Chelfham Barton, Bratton Fleming, Blackmore Gate and here we are nearly 1000ft high, then a drop to Parracombe. We then get some delightful scenes to Woody Bay and from here to Lynton it surpasses all, the West Lynn beneath and Barbrook Mill village with glorious woods giving a delightfully cooling effect.

Figure 44: *Lynmouth, Mars Hill*

We are over 1000ft as we approach Lynton. We ascend a very steep hill from the station, called Sinai Hill, and arrive at Waterloo House, Lydiate Lane. After dinner took a short walk. The town is a fair size and grand views are obtained everywhere. We took the cliff walk to Lynmouth, getting delightful views of the valley as we wound down the narrow path. Lynmouth is in a valley at the mouth of the Lynn between precipitous hills with quaint little houses, Mars Hill being most charmingly quaint, this in particular took Sissie's fancy. There is a nice promenade, the hotels are dotted here and there amongst the trees and appear to be built on a ledge. They are very imposing, with magnificent gardens.

There is a small jetty with a quaint Rhenish Tower erected, an exact copy of one on the Rhine. This is at the foot of Mars Hill and so corresponds in style. The tower is over 100 years old. The East and West Lynn rushing beneath and flowing into the sea makes it an ideal spot. A charming little bridge spans the Lynn. We took the lift up to Lynton as we were too tired to climb, then to bed.

Sunday

Delightful morning, had a short stroll round Lynton. There are many quaint narrow little streets made in such irregular order, leading in many cases to the sweetest of houses. The church is interesting, especially the village stocks which are to be seen in the churchyard. We found our way to the Valley of Rocks and there spent a perfectly delightful morning lying on the cliffs just above North Walk.

The sea was a grand sight, such a perfect blue and so calm and still. A typical Sabbath Morn and we read some *Jeremiah*.

The rocks are lovely and the coast is very rugged, looks so majestic against the tranquil sea. After dinner took a walk up Sinai Hill and strolled into the garden of an empty house. We got a delightful view, woods covering the hills and the perfect blue of the sea and purple-clad hills, with the rushing Lynn beneath, making a perfect picture.

After tea to the Wesleyan Methodist Chapel and at 8 o'clock the

Congregational Choir gave a song service outside the Town Hall. It was lovely to hear the well-known hymns such as *Eternal Father* and *Giver of All* sung with such enthusiasm in this delightful spot.

Monday

Not much sun but quite fine all day. Had a charming walk up to Hollerday Hill. Taking the road by the Town Hall, up the hydrangea walk to George Newnes House (practically destroyed last August by suffragettes).

The house occupies a splendid position and the view on the top of the hill is magnificent. The road leading up to it is very steep, on either side a profusion of hydrangea, very fine blossoms and gorgeous colourings. A splendid view is obtained of Countisbury Foreland and Woody Bay with a marvellous expanse of coast scenery and the downs rising behind. We spent the whole morning on the top of the downs. The sea was very calm and rather misty so that we were not able to see the Welsh coast which, on a clear day, is said to be visible.

Figure 45: *Watersmeet and Cottage*

The downs are covered with lovely heather and gorse. We spent a lazy time and came home through some delightful woods to North Walk then home to lunch. After lunch took lift to Lynmouth and proceeded up the East Lynn to Watersmeet, situated between Countisbury Hill and Summerhouse Hill.

It is a most charming sight, and we walked for 2½ miles amongst the wooded gorge with glorious hills rising to nearly 1000ft, thickly wooded, and the rushing Lynn beneath. We rested on the rocks and so were able to enjoy all the beauties surrounding us. The waters of the Lynn are utilised to generate the electricity for Lynton and Lynmouth. At places the stream is quite narrow and then emerges into quite a wide river, the path leads sometimes level and other times it is 50ft above the water. Hawkseen Tors rise on the right to 935ft and are heather-clad.

We continue the path until we reach Myrtleberry Cottage and there partake of a lovely Devonshire tea in a delightful garden surrounded with hills. After tea we resume our walk for 5 minutes to Watersmeet. Here the East Lynn is met by the foaming Combe Park Water. We climbed up some distance into the woods and had a most magnificent view. We then with regret were forced to turn our footsteps home, promising ourselves another visit in a day or two. We took the road home, which is much nearer and also a change of scenery, arriving home for dinner at 7.30pm. After dinner sat in a secluded spot on North Walk, then to bed 10 o'clock.

Tuesday

Lovely sunny day, walked to Valley of Rocks. Spent the morning on Ragged Jack. Sis felt a little weary so had a rest and I did some climbing. The peaks are very jagged and it is a delightful sight to sit on one of them and take in the view of the rugged cliffs beneath with the sea below. The North Walk runs right along the face of the cliff and it is a very sheltered spot, but we like to get to the top and a good blow. After lunch a stroll round the town, and in the evening before dinner we took the private path of the Royal Castle Hotel grounds to

Lynmouth and here obtained a most magnificent view.

The view of the bay is perfectly lovely and the colourings were just shown up to perfection, the beautiful red cliffs of Countisbury looking charming with its heather-clad summit and the East Lynn beneath. Then, rising to the right of East Lynn is Summerhouse Hill with the wooded Glen Lynn at its base. Beyond lay Sinai Hill and at the back Hollerday Hill, a charming sight, the beautiful colourings so greatly adding to its beauty. We sat on the beach for some time then back to dinner at 9.30pm and after dinner a stroll through the Valley of Rocks Hotel grounds to North Walk.

Sat and watched the flashlight from Countisbury Foreland lighthouse and the lights on the Welsh coast. Most perfect night, the moon hidden by the hills. Walked to the Valley of Rocks and there a grand sight presented itself. The whole valley flooded in moonlight, and here and there the shadow of the hills and the sea beyond. A sight we both shall never forget. We are not only getting grand days but perfect moonlight nights. Had a hard job to get Sis away, not saying how loth I myself was to leave it.

Wednesday

Grand day again. Took our lunch and prepared for a day on the downs. Went up the Red Road, Countisbury Hill, from Lynmouth. We had a long cliff climb of about 1½ miles to the village of Countisbury, on our way seeing in the distance the sweet bay called Sillery Sands. Fair amount of people bathing and it looks very inviting. It was simply baking and we found it very hot after a long tramp. We turned on to the downs and sat amongst the heather. The hill we think is called Kipscombe. We enjoyed a long rest and then for the next two hours roamed about on the downs getting some grand views of the coast and in the distance range upon range of the Exmoor Hills making a most marvellous panorama, one never to be forgotten. On our left we could see the Valley of the Lynn and even the rushing water in places. We determine to make for the Foreland Lighthouse but it was some hours before we arrived there. In fact we lost our way and had at last to climb down a very dangerous and rugged hill with only a sheep track to guide us. We did not see a human being or house and a great longing for tea came over us. It was a welcome sight to see a little house attached to the lighthouse and after enquiries found they could give us some tea. We had great kindness shown us and we did good justice to the tea.

Figure 46: *Foreland Lighthouse*

It is a lovely spot with nothing but blue sea around. The character of the light is four flashes every fifteen seconds and is 56,750 candlepower. Lynmouth Bay lies at the left and cliffs rising to Hollerday Hill in the distance, and Castle Rock standing out in prominence. On our right lies Coddow Combe and Porlock Bay.

We turned our steps homeward, luckily were put onto the right path. The walk from here is charming, such a lovely rugged coast, and the hills are golden with the gorse and purple with the heather, the cliffs a lovely red making a perfect sight. No wonder this hill looks to be so grand in colour when we view it from Lynton.

On arriving at Countisbury Church, we take the main road and get a steep descent to Lynmouth and here again get another different view of

Lynton and it is indeed grand. The hills rising covered with soft foliage and here and there houses placed in most obscure places. After dinner a walk along North Walk and another charming sight of the Valley of Rocks flooded with moonlight. Sis would not leave it and I had to pull her home to bed.

Thursday

Grand day and very hot. Took the lift to Lynmouth and then boarded one of the little boats to meet the steamer en route for Clovelly. We had a grand trip and fairly good views of the coast, although rather misty. The Castle Rock looked very imposing, then on to Duty Point, Woody Bay (very charming), and Heddon's Mouth. Saw Watermouth Castle just by Burrow Nose, then Hele Bay, Hillsborough and on to Ilfracombe. There appeared to be many people on Lantern Hill and Capstone. Our next point of interest was Bull Point with its lighthouse, Morte Point at the beginning of Woolacombe Sands, Baggy Point and then on to Clovelly.

Figure 47: *Clovelly*

We landed in little boats and climbed the narrow but very steep little street of one mile in length. It is indeed a quaint and particularly charming spot and we were privileged in seeing it under the very best conditions.

There are charming little houses with fuchsias in abundance and the little street is made of cobblestones, very trying, especially on a hot day but above all "there is a Wesleyan Chapel!" We had a glorious drive round the noted Hobby Drive. The road was made by one of the noted Hamley family about eighty years ago. It is cut on the hills and goes in and out amongst the little valleys for three miles.

We then turned into the main road and came to a little church which is very interesting indeed. The pulpit base is made of rock from Lundy Island and there is a monument to Charles Kingsley, whose brother-in-law was once vicar here. The Hamley house is adjoining the church, an inscription on the lodge says 'Go East, Go West, Home is best'. After a nice tea in a quaint cottage, had a lovely sail home, the cliffs looking lovely and more clear than in the morning. A glorious sunset like a ball of fire shining in the water and we landed before it had vanished and at Hollerday Hill it was lost to sight. A moonlight walk in Valley of Rocks and to bed 10 o'clock.

Friday

Had a lazy morning sat in the Valley of Rocks. After lunch walked to Barbrook Mill village by way of Barnstaple Road. We passed the gorge of the West Lynn and through Lynbridge. The village of Barbrook is very sweet with soft scenery and a little stream running through. Beggars Roost Hill rises on the left to over 1000ft. We turned from the main road, leaving the river on our left and soon get to the downs through the hamlet of Dean to Mount Sinai, 1000ft. The view here is magnificent, hill upon hill rising everywhere, the many shades of colourings giving a most charming effect, the Exmoor Downs away in the distance. We descend to Lynton by Lydiate Lane, tea at the Greenhouse Tea Rooms. After dinner to the Valley of Rocks but the moon was not so brilliant, many clouds about.

Saturday

Delightful walk to Hunters Inn, en route passing through the Valley of Rocks, with South Cleave rising on our left and Mother Meldrum's Cave. Passing Wringcliff Bay we come to Duty Point. Here we pass into the private demesne of Lee Abbey, an ideal place in the trees, and woods rising up to Duty Point with its tower surmounting it. Here, if one is privileged, a grand view is obtained, but we had to admire it at a distance. We pass on to Lee Bay and it is so inviting that we promise ourselves a day there.

Figure 48: *Hunters Inn*

After walking through some lovely woods we come to Woody Bay. Trees rise on the hills to a great height and the bay is charming. Several houses are built on the hills within easy reach of the sea but our most charming view was still to come. We took the cliff path from Woody Bay to Heddon's Mouth and for two miles walk on a narrow path high up the cliff. There is seen Countisbury Foreland with its lighthouse, Lynmouth Bay, and Castle Rock looking most imposing, Lee Bay and Woody Bay, with its rugged coast and the water tumbling in and out.

Heddon's Mouth is very different from the scenery we have passed through. Peter Rock is a barren and desolate hill rising to the right and the pretty Heddon River beneath. After an enjoyable rest by the river we follow its course to Hunter's Inn. This is a delightful place. The only house practically is the Inn and it is situated in a valley with wonderful wooded hills rising all round. We took a stroll to Trentishoe Combe and then enjoyed a good tea of cream and jam at the inn. Our walk home was by way of Killington, Parracombe Cross, passing Woody Bay station to Caffyns Heanton Cross, then join Lydiate Lane and back to dinner at 7.30, after seeing some of the most charming of scenery. Really did not think that Devon held such beauties, although I always imagined it lovely, but this surpasses my expectations and the colouring and berries of the various trees are simply superb.

Sunday

Another grand day. Walked up to Hollerday Hill, through the Lydiardgean walk, getting wonderful view of the coast and Lynmouth. A delightful breeze, but almost too cool to be pleasant. Came home by the Valley of Rocks side, but had such a dangerous descent that we did not enjoy it at all. It was not worth all the scratches and falls which we had. Walked home via South Cleave. After lunch found 'Fairholm', it looks to have a most unique position and a grand view obtained of Lynmouth and coast. Walked along North Walk and Valley of Rocks. This appeals to us both so much and grows more imposing in character with Woody Bay and Lee Bay in the distance.

Service at 7.30 at Congregational Chapel and then enjoyed a stroll and talk and also listened to the sweet singing of hymns at the Town Hall. Our favourite sung, *Dear Lord and Father of Mankind*.

Monday

Walked to Lee Bay and had a bathe. It is a lovely little spot with beautiful sands, the water was grand and we thoroughly enjoyed our dip. The bay is very rugged, huge rocks and boulders, with Duty Point rising covered with trees. Looking up towards the Abbey there is a charming view of a lovely greensward. Walked to Woody Bay and had tea at the Post Office overlooking the bay. Martinhoe Manor, a lovely house commanding a grand view of the coast.

We then climbed up to Martinhoe Common, 1000ft. It is just perfect with heather and gorse in profusion. Away in the distance is a grand view of the Foreland, Castle Rock and many other points of interest. Had such a blow to Woody Bay Station, it really was charming, at every point some fresh interest awaits us.

At Lynton we watched a party of French people arrive by train and were relating, we imagined, to their relatives who met them the events of the war. After dinner, sat on the balcony until bedtime.

Tuesday

Very high wind and rather rough. Rained hard in the night but turned out another lovely day. Much clearer than we have previously had. Took coach to Malmsmead, leaving Lynton 11 o'clock and proceeding down the noted Lynton Hill. Charming views are obtained of Glen Lynn, but so much of the pleasure is taken away by the fact that one has to hold on for dear life hoping to arrive safely at the bottom. From the Lyndale Hotel, we took the Watersmeet Road, passing the same route as last week. We get glimpses of the water beneath with the hills rising on either side, a wooded gorge, almost unimaginable beauty. At Watersmeet we follow the Combe Park Water, Farley Water to Hillsford Bridge, this is very lovely. We then have a steep climb on foot and then descend from Brendon Church School, getting a lovely view of Rockford. We stay a few minutes at Rockford Inn then proceed to Millslade and Malmsmead.

Figure 49: *Badgworthy Valley*

Here we alight and, finding that we have three hours at our disposal, decide to walk to the Doone Valley by way of Badgworthy Water. The Badgworthy Valley is perfectly charming, we think it surpasses all else we have yet seen. After passing Lorna Doone's Bower, we walk by the river for about 2½ miles. This is said to be the most striking glen in Exmoor. From the river the land rises steeply on either side, in some parts wooded, but on the whole very bare and covered with gorse and heather, the colourings superb. After walking for some time we come to Coombe Water, cross a very rocky bridge and follow the valley up to Doone Valley, passing again through lovely scenery. The Doone Valley is very bare, not nearly as pretty as the Badgworthy Valley.

Figure 50: *Countisbury Hill and Lynmouth*

We had to return quickly and take coach to Oare, visiting the church where Lorna Doone is said to have been shot at during her marriage service. Taking the road again we climb a steep hill, road quite red, the view is very extensive and magnificent, quite one of the finest I have ever seen, the hills gorgeously clad in colour and wooded.

On our right lay Brendon and below Malmsmead, and to the left Oare and East Lynn (now become Oare Water). We are now on the moors and get a lovely view of the sea and Welsh coast. It is very clear. We pass the County Gate with the valley of Glenthorne on our right. Then a delightful drive on the moors to Countisbury and down the noted steep hill to Lynmouth, obtaining a charming view of the bay and Lynton. Sat on Castle Rock and watched the sunset. Saw the sun dip into the sea and disappear, leaving everything looking red, ourselves included. We then cantered home to dinner as fast as we could.

Wednesday

Started early for a long walk, taking lunch with us. Walked to Watersmeet, then by the side of the Combe Park water to Hillsford Bridge. This river is much more narrow and very thickly wooded, and the ferns and trees and colouring are more than my pen can hope to describe. We take the same road as previously to Brendon Church, then by the fields to Rockford and so get a very charming view of the Rockford Valley, East Lynn hidden by the trees. We walked by the East Lynn to Millslade.

Rain came on and we retraced our steps, having a good tea on the way at Rockford Inn with enough cream to satisfy even Sis, saying not a word about myself. The East Lynn is indeed charming and we follow it to Lynmouth. At every turn is some new charm and we stop many times to watch some sweet spot but 'ere we have gone far something even more charming appears. The trees looking so green from the rain and the air so fresh and cool, with the water bubbling and foaming beneath amongst huge boulders. The view of Lynmouth approached from East Lynn is sweet with the little houses on Mars Hill and Rhenish Tower in front. We walked up to Lynton in the pouring rain and experienced our first wet night. Stay in and have some music.

Thursday

Very dull first thing and a lot of rain fell in the night but it cleared up beautifully and we spent a very enjoyable morning. Everything seemed so lovely and fresh and we enjoyed the change. Walking along North Walk we had a charming view of the Lynn foaming and rushing tremendously after the heavy rain. Such a charming sight, the sea appeared to be affected so the water for some distance was thick with mud by the effects of the Lynn and beyond this was a perfect blue and over Countisbury the sun was shining, throwing up all its grand colouring. We spent the morning on Castle Rock, the sun very hot and no air.

After lunch went down to Lynmouth to see Glen Lynn. There was a huge volume of water. It is indeed sweet and the water falls from a good height and quite a steep climb to the end of the glen. Beautiful soft trees fall into the water and there are ferns in abundance of all varieties. The spray from the falls threatened to give us a fair soaking and as the rain came we turned our steps and walked back to Waterloo House for tea instead of the Bath Hotel as we had intended.

With much regret and great longings for more of Lynton, we were forced to bid farewell and turn our steps to that terrible hill and make for the station. We had three quarters of an hour to wait so were able to look again on the beauties of Lynton and Lynmouth, agreeing that they hold scenes which cannot be surpassed, and delights and pleasant memories of happy hours spent in their valleys which will ever remain in our memories. We go away richer in many ways than we came, although pockets considerably lighter.

Took train to Barnstaple, the moors thick with mist and we got no view at all en route. Put up at the Waverley Hotel, Ivy Street, and at once felt very comfortable and at home.

Friday

Spent the morning looking round Barnstaple. Friday is Market Day and we found the market in High Street to be very interesting. Crowds of people buying and selling all kinds of produce, cream, butter, eggs, poultry and many other things, all looking particularly clean and appetising. There was also a lot of Barum ware for sale. On our way to The Parade we passed the clock tower built to commemorate the Prince Consort.

From here we walked through the park and down Barbican Street, an exceedingly interesting item was a visit to the Golden Lion Hotel,

Boutport Street. The ceilings are decorated in Italian plaster and is most beautiful work.

We passed the noted Barum shop, Litchdon Street, with its huge display of ware but we resisted the temptation and walked on the Penrose Almshouses, built nearly 300 years ago and given by a Mr Penrose who also left 2/6 a week for each inhabitant.

Figure 51: *Penrose Almshouses, Barnstaple*

There is also a church adjoining, where the inmates must attend once a day for prayers. We found them to be very interesting and pretty, especially the little courtyard with a pump in the centre being most picturesque. The Parish Church contains some very old memorials, one in particular being very beautiful, that of Richard Beaple.

We then crossed the long bridge which spans the River Taw, called Barnstaple Bridge, and took train for Bideford. Just at the station we fell into the Carters, had a few words and hoped to see them at Exmouth. We pass en route the station of Fremington, where the clay is produced for making the ware, then on to Instow with Appledore opposite, Braunton

Burrows across the river, which is now the Torridge.

We walk across the very noted bridge of Bideford and have a walk round the town. It is a very pretty little town built on a hill rising on either side of the river. The river is very wide and the hills rise above it, well studded with trees. The streets are very quaint and narrow, many only little alleys but all very clean. The Victoria Park is exceedingly pretty and situated by the riverside.

Figure 52: *Statue of Charles Kingsley*

At the entrance is a splendid statue of Charles Kingsley, who looks such a noble man. The church contains some old memorials restored from the original Parish Church (dated 1630) and there are some beautiful stained glass windows, also a memorial to Richard Grenville of the *Revenge*. After visiting the Atheneum we crossed the bridge and went into the Royal Hotel and there saw the room where Charles Kingsley wrote *Westward Ho*. It is a lovely old room and contains some interesting prints, also a letter written by Charles Kingsley himself. Train to Barnstaple arriving 6 o'clock. Tea at Pearses and an evening in writing.

Saturday

After breakfast we walked to Queen Anne's Walk and then round Boutport Street to Pilton. Pilton is a very pretty little place, the High Street in particular being very picturesque with its old Church House sign hanging out. There are some pretty almshouses surrounding the church which have recently been rebuilt, replacing some very old ones. The church is entirely surrounded by houses and is really very beautiful, the tower in particular being very handsome. There are traces of older buildings on the outside wall, said to have once been a monastery.

The interior contains one of the finest of screens but sadly in need of repair and there is a beautiful font with a very handsome cover. There are also some fine memorials, one to a family named Blake being very beautiful. On our way back to Barnstaple we visited the Barum pottery and watched with great interest the actual clay being made into jugs and pots, then following on to the painting, glazing, etc., until the article is ready for sale. After lunch took train to Exeter and spent a short time in the Cathedral. Not long enough to see all its beauties, as it needs quite a day (Sis would say a week), but long enough to be greatly impressed with the magnificence of its pillars and screens. Hope to visit it again and have longer time in it. The exterior is fine but has to my idea not sufficient space to show off its beauty to perfection. Took 6.15 train to Exmouth, Gertie and Hettie met us and after tea we had a walk on the Maer and a lovely blow by the sea.

Sunday

Walked to Point-in-View Chapel, a sweet little place, would seat only about 30 people.

Figure 53: *Point-in-View Chapel*

A charity was left providing this chapel, together with some houses and the inmates used this as their place of worship. The view is very fine and it is indeed a choice spot to choose. The hills rise in the distance and below them runs the River Exe. After dinner walked along the Beacon and sat by the sea. The sands are very extensive and the view very good, Teignmouth, Dawlish, etc., on the right. The scenery is very different from North Devon, not so fine but very pretty. In the evening had a very enjoyable service at the Congregational Chapel and the sermon Sis and I both enjoyed immensely. After service, we had a nice singsong of favourite hymns.

Monday

Very windy day. Walked to Orcombe Point and sat on the rocks. It is a nice little bay, all the rocks and cliffs are red and a nice sandy beach. We had a most enjoyable morning, the sea looked glorious and fairly rough. Had a fearfully windy walk home, the two weak ones, Gertie and Sis, feeling very done up.

The afternoon was very exciting. Spent it on the railway station, met the 2.54 but Sis's mother did not arrive. Saw Gertie leave by the 3.30 and then waited for 4.02 and not in vain. So we walked joyously home to tea. Sis, Het and I had a nice walk to the front in the evening and we all so much enjoyed it.

Tuesday

Took train to Budleigh Salterton and had such a perfectly lovely day. It is a sweet little place with a little stream running through the principal street. There is a fine expanse of sea and the cliffs are red rising on either side.

We sat quite on the edge of the beach (which is pebble) for about two hours and enjoyed a real lazy time. Also had our lunch. Sis, Het and I went for a walk by the Otter, up the Otter valley, very pretty, especially higher up the valley. We came back to a lovely tea, such a spread in a little room all to ourselves. Our walk home over the cliffs to Exmouth was indeed one of the finest. There is such a perfect view high on the cliff of Budleigh Salterton and away in the distance miles of cultivated land, a marvellous panorama. We could see a range of white cliffs on our right, probably Sidmouth or Seaton. We feasted our eyes on the scene for a long time until the fading of daylight reminded us that we must not loiter.

After passing over the highest point we obtained a grand view of the sunset over the Haldon Hills bathed in gold, too perfect for words, then below lay the River Exe. We passed Straight Point and Orcombe Point and then Exmouth, after all pronouncing it a lovely day.

Wednesday

Took train to Topsham and crossed by the ferry over the River Exe and by bridge over the canal for Exminster. Topsham is one of the oldest towns and where Drake is said to have hailed from.

After walking over the marshes and through the village we arrived at the farm where Hettie's friends live. The orchards were strewn with fruit and we had more than we could wish for, the trees literally laden. Had some rather good views from the surrounding country. Caught the 7.40 train and home at 8.00. In the evening Lecture No. 1 to Sis, taken I think seriously. Whether it is acted upon remains to be proved.

Thursday

Walked through Phear Park to Withycombe in the morning. Came home. Het and I walked to the seafront and Het had her last blow by the sea and it was a real good one. Sea very rough and we had a hard job to fight against the wind. Our first good sea, I did enjoy it. After dinner saw Het off and the rest of the time we spent by the sea. In the evening Sis and I had a delightful walk and talk then home to bed.

Friday

Took train to Budleigh Salterton and had a nice time on the beach and enjoyed the sea, such a lovely day. We discovered that salt at one time was made here, hence the name Salterton, taken from 'Saltpan'. The little house, octagon-shape, near the beach, is where J. Millais painted the picture 'Childhood of Walter Raleigh', and the wall opposite is shown in the picture.

Figure 54: *Boyhood of Raleigh, by J. Millais*

The home of Walter Raleigh is Hayes Barton, quite near.

We walked to Otterton and visited the church, recently rebuilt by Lady Rolle. Back by Otterton Park and had such a lovely view of the Otter Valley. After tea spent the evening on the front, very wet, so we had to take train home.

Saturday

Our last morning so we spent it on the beach. Such a lovely day and we were very loth to have to leave the sea but the pangs of hunger called us back to material things. After dinner caught the 3.35 train. So nice to feel Sis and I could return together and we had a very nice journey to finish up an exceedingly happy holiday spent in choice company and scenery. It was with sad hearts, and yet glad in other things, that we reluctantly turned our backs on it to take up again with renewed energies the daily round, feeling it to be a pleasure after such a long restful and happy time.

7.

August/September 1915
A holiday in Cornwall

Saturday August 21st

We (Eva and I) left Paddington by 10.30 express to Exeter, arriving at 1.35, where Hettie and Olive met us. We spent a very pleasant hour with them, having a light lunch at the Temperance Hotel (rotten). At 2.35 we continued our journey, which was exceedingly comfortable throughout and full of interest, especially beyond Exeter. Here we travelled beside the Exe and gazed again on dear familiar Exmouth and its environs where we spent so happy a week last year.

As we passed The Warren on to Dawlish the view broadened and the lovely red cliffs beyond Exmouth with Orcombe Point were in sight. It was our first view of the sea, which was grand, a perfect blue with a glorious background of red rocks and grass-crowned cliffs stretching away on our right towards Torquay. Dawlish is of course spoilt for itself by the railway running across its very front, but the entranced passers-by benefit.

Passing Teignmouth, we now turn inland beside the River Teign and view the beauty of Shaldon and the surrounding hills and valleys and lovely greenswards which reach to the water's edge till we reach Newton Abbot, the edge of Dartmoor. Then at Totnes, we cross the Dart and now enter (to me) a new country. Rivers abound and the valleys are deep ravines, tree-clad, of great beauty. We pass Ivybridge and on to Devonport and Plymouth, crossing the bridge at Saltash. Many boats and ships were on the rivers here.

We had tea on the train just before reaching Par, where carriages are slipped, the first portion going on to Penzance. We had a short stroll on the platform and heard the stationmaster speak in true Devonian brogue. Continuing, we passed some quaint little stations, one St Columb Road (seven miles from St Columb Minor, our destination). The country is very charming, moorland scenery as we near Newquay with the rocky coast in the distance. A trap awaited us and we drove (1½ miles) to our abode for a fortnight, Cross Mount, St Columb Minor.

Figure 55: *Cross Mount, St Columb Minor*

A charming house (originally two cottages) but added to from time to time, not thereby losing its old-fashioned charm which was very considerably accentuated on entering and on further acquaintance. Lovely old china and bowls of perfect sweet peas everywhere. The centre front of the house is almost entirely of glass and the garden, though small, has some very nice flowers.

The village is very small, but quite a large church, which is still the parish church of Newquay and years ago St Columb was the principal place but the railway has brought Newquay into prominence.

Sunday

Taking the road to the left of the church we cross three fields and down a little lane to the Porth beach. From the fields we command a magnificent view of the Porth with Newquay on the left and to the right stretch miles of country. We were especially charmed with the few houses and lovely gardens on our way to the bay. We spent some time on the sands which are very lovely and stretch for about 3 miles. There is indeed a great expanse with huge rocks and boulders scattered about.

We then climbed Trevelgue Head – *our* headland – owned by Lady Tangye (but later given by her to the public) whose house, Glendorgal, is beautifully situated opposite. The coast on our right is very lovely. There appear to be many little bays with lovely stretches of sand surrounded by high jagged cliffs. A glorious Sabbath morn and we read and talked on the great Theme.

After dinner we sat in the fields at the top of our road, and in the evening went to the Wesleyan chapel in the village where the singing, if not sweet, was certainly inspiring by the heartiness in which all joined. It was a very nice service which we both enjoyed. After chapel, a delightful stroll to see the sunset. It was a grand sight, the sun dipping over the sea until it was lost in the horizon. It vanished so quickly as with the turn of an electric switch. The afterglow was even more beautiful, the country all around being bathed in the lovely soft rose colour whilst in the midst of all was the rising moon. We took our fill of its beauty and turned our steps homeward.

Monday

After breakfast we made for Porth Beach, the walk to it over the fields is indeed delightful. Beyond Newquay on the right is Towan Head where the Headland Hotel is situated, and on the right miles of cultivated country with Watergate Bay village and hotel at the water's edge, and then miles of coast scenery of the wildest beauty to Trevose Head and lighthouse. We had a delightful bathe. Found a nice quiet little spot, there being no such marks of civilisation as machines.

Figure 56: *Watergate Bay and Hotel*

The sea was very calm and the lovely sand made it very enjoyable. We climbed the steep cliff of Lusty Glaze Beach and had a lovely walk home. After lunch took the field path to Newquay but were disappointed to find ourselves so soon on the road. We were not particularly taken with Newquay itself, the rocks and bays are of course lovely but our fancy is not for <u>towns</u>. A lovely walk back over the cliff to Porth, such charming views of coast and country, the sea a deep blue enhanced by the yellow sand and rugged coastlines.

Tea at the tearooms on the beach owned by our Mrs. Roberts, so it is a second home to drop into. We then sat on the cliff opposite the Norwegian Rock until we felt quite chilly. The colouring of the fast-approaching sunset threw up all the beauty around and on our way home we stayed at intervals to look back on such a perfect scene. We reluctantly turned in to dinner (to which however we did ample justice) and later strolled to a little hill at the back of the village to see the whole landscape flooded in glorious moonlight.

Tuesday

At 9.30 started for a long tramp taking lunch. We followed the St Columb Major road as far as the Carnanton woods getting en route some good extensive views, seeing at one point towards Bodmin, some Cornish tin mines. We were greatly disappointed to find the woods closed during the war. They looked so inviting. However, we found a side track which we followed some little way. The bracken was sweetly pretty and the softness of the green foliage perfection and the scents of the woods brought out by apparently recent rain.

Figure 57: *Mawgan Church*

Reached St Mawgan at 1.30, a very pretty village said to be the gem of all North Cornwall's scenery. The church is very interesting, containing some old brasses, well preserved, and some fine oak carving. Pamphlets with particulars of the church are placed for the use of visitors. In the churchyard are two very old Cornish crosses, one particularly interesting. We endeavoured also to see the Chapel of the Nunnery, which latter is situated quite close to the church but the nuns were at vespers and we could not be admitted till 3.00 so did not feel inclined to wait.

We made our way through the Vale of Lanherne to Mawgan Porth – no road this time but field paths and common. The view of Mawgan as you leave it is very beautiful, nestling among the trees with its beautiful church and nunnery (which was an old mansion of the Arundell family). The Porth was charming, the sand even finer than in the other bays and so firm that we could not resist the temptation of a paddle. We then scrambled up a steep cliff path and made our way to Watergate Bay. We could see the rocks which lie beyond Newquay to Pentire Point East.

As we wended our way along many different views of the coast appeared, the caves and rocks making a charming picture with the deep blue of the sea against the ruggedness of the cliffs. For miles this gorgeous vision extended. No words can do it justice. A welcome tea of splits and cream at Watergate Bay preceded the final stage of our walk over the cliffs to Porth. Here at one spot the heather and gorse in bloom added a greater wealth of colour to the scene which was already taking on the beautiful softened tints of early evening. Home at 7 o'clock rather tired.

Wednesday

Spent the morning in the Porth. Bathed and generally had a lazy time. We peeped in some of the caves but they looked very weird and do not entice either of us. Some are very huge. It was however delightful to spend the time on the sands, wandering round the rocks and doing a bit of climbing. Went up to Cross Mount to lunch and still not energetic we rested for a little while, getting down to Porth just in time for tea, after which we walked onto the headland and found a spot near to the Norwegian Rock where we spent a quiet and enjoyable time knitting, reading and watching the brilliant colourings of the sea as it dashed around the rocks which towered in irregular piles some near, some far, whilst in the caves beneath us it sounded like thunder.

Figure 58: *Porth Sands*

After dinner we walked into Newquay and heard a fine organ recital by Mr Tonkin at the Wesleyan Church. Madame Strathearn sang *Land of Hope and Glory* and Braga's *Serenata*, the accomplished organist playing the violin accompaniment whilst a Belgian refugee (lady) played the organ. We also heard a duet on the organ which was quite unique. The walk home was grandeur itself, the country and sea bathed in brilliant moonlight 'calm and still'.

Figure 59: *Huer's Hut, Newquay*

Thursday

Walked to Newquay on the sands after waiting a little while for the tide to serve. We passed Criggars and Tolcarne Beaches, the Great Western Beach and the Towan Beach to the natural harbour by which we ascended to the town. We do not think any of these beaches come up to St Columb Porth for which our affection is daily growing. We made our way to Towan Head which runs for nearly a mile out to sea, passing on our way the Huer's Lookout House, a symbol of a departed industry – the lookout being for 'shoals of pilchards'.

This is near the Atlantic Hotel, and we pass on to the extreme point from whence the sweep of coastline is wonderful, the dark perpendicular cliffs showing prominently above the yellow sands and the blue sea. First could be seen Newquay, then Porth, then Watergate Bay and on to Mawgan (all points we know now) and beyond the Bedruthan Rocks (yet to be visited) and away to Trevose Head. On our left is an unexplored country but here immediately below us are the great boulders of Fistral Bay, which stretches in a semi-circle for some distance away to Pentire Point East. The Towan headland is beautiful (still not so much as Trevelgue, our headland at Porth).

We now descended and clambered over rocks to reach the other side of Fistral Bay in which there is a glorious stretch of sand. The rocks are magnificent – it is said the Atlantic hurls itself among these boulders with tremendous power (the endeavour to build a pier being futile). We both feel how grand a sight a rough sea would be here. Crossing the bay we climbed the cliff and crossed East Pentire Point, and came unexpectedly on the beauty of the Gannel Estuary, its placid waters and the soft foliage on both points (East and West Pentire) being in marked contrast to the scene we have just left. We found a spot for tea which overlooked this restful scene and the welcomeness of the Cornish fare was very much added to by the vision spread before us. Body and soul alike fed and were filled.

It is possible to cross the Gannel by a footbridge at low tide and on our way home we turned down a lane and crossed some fields to find it, but evidently it was already covered by the incoming tide. Our return was by way of Mount Wise and Bank Street, by the Wesleyan Chapel and then the road to St Columb Minor.

Friday

Figure 60: *Trerice Manor*

Spent the whole morning in a field near the house where we could command an extensive view of the country with Porth a little to our left and the wide expanse of sea and cliffs. After lunch we walked to Trerice Manor with Mrs Holland passing Quintrell Downs Halt and Kestle Mill by which latter we crossed the Gannel – here a mere stream. Turning sharply to our right we enter a beautiful lane, the trees meeting overhead (a welcome shade from the sun) and the hedges and ditches full of soft foliage and ferns of all varieties in abundance. As we neared the Manor the road became even more beautiful, fruit trees all along the hedges. Evidently the road had been cut through an orchard and the trees were degenerating towards a wild state.

The old Manor was very interesting, being built in 1572–3, these dates being over the fireplace. Only two rooms are on view – the dining hall and drawing room. In the former there is a window with no fewer than 576 panes of glass and minstrel's gallery extends the length of the hall. In the drawing room there is a fine Italian plaster ceiling and an old table of black oak – the top a solid plank – said to have been in the house 300 years. The coats of arms of the Arundell family (the original owners) and the Duke of Cornwall are on the wall. A fine old garden surrounds the house with fine fruit and flowers, and I was stung on the ear by a bee for looking too longingly at the peaches. Taking the same route home we stayed at the Trewarne Tea Gardens for tea. We not only had a good tea but most charming hospitality, for the lady of the house brought us hammocks and cushions to rest in and gave us a bunch of lovely flowers as a send-off home.

Saturday

Spent the morning on Trevelgue headland and had a delightful view of the coast round Watergate Bay and on to Trevose Head. The sea and sky were the bluest of blues and the beautiful colourings of the cliffs were thrown up, the waves playing and foaming among the rocks. I sat and wrote to Fred (who had just left for the front) whilst Eva bathed in a cave opposite Norwegian Rock. In the afternoon we scrambled over hedges and ditches (and trespassed) in our attempt to find a short cut to the tea house. We had a pretty walk along the stream which runs into Porth but had to acknowledge that the way was not a nearer one. After tea we climbed the cliff near Zacry's Island, the colourings of the sea had changed since the morning and were now a deep blue. Clouds were hovering round but they dispersed that we might take another store of pictures for our future refreshment of the indescribable beauty which surrounded us. We read some of *Sir Gibbie* by George MacDonald. A cold wind was blowing and we were forced to put on our coats and take a sharp walk. Of course it was again onto the headland and we were fortunate in discovering the 'Blowing Hole', but the sea was rather calm and the effect was not the best.

As we climbed the fields towards home we, as always, turned and viewed with charmed eyes and hearts the beautiful Porth.

Sunday

Figure 61: *Norwegian Rock*

We awoke to the sound of raindrops (heavy ones), the first clouded morning. We started for a walk before church and found it delightfully breezy and decided to walk into Newquay to the Wesleyan Chapel. Our way lay over the cliffs that we might not lose any aspect of beauty which might be ours of the sea and rocks, and this morning the sea was much rougher and grander. The service was very enjoyable and the music and singing very good (saw Norman Sargent from Archway there). We had a very windy walk home by the cliffs.

Sat in the garden all the afternoon. After tea strolled round the village, found Mrs. Roberts' garden. Attended the service at St Columb Minor Parish Church (subject Gehazi 'Went not my heart with thee',

2 Kings V, 26). The singing here was very poor. Coming out we saw the afterglow of a very fine sunset and hurrying down to the Porth found the sea truly rough. We walked right onto the headland, crossing the Porth Bridge, under which huge waves rolled and roared on the rocks.

We stayed a while to watch it and to get a view of the coast under these fascinating conditions – the sky being now red and gold and the sea a deep green. We were very glad indeed to have been privileged to see a rough sea on this wonderful coast. 'How wonderful are thy works, O Lord.'

Monday

A very fresh morning, but beautifully clear. We anticipate another lovely week for weather. Walked into Newquay, took the rail motor to Perranporth. A very pretty run via Trerice, Newlyn and Goonhavern. The scenery was particularly soft as we neared Perranporth, the hills around very steep, and here and there appear some kind of quarries, or probably disused mines. The village lies in a valley and is a trifle disappointing after the immediate approach. The houses too are not pretty, but the sands are lovely. They are said to stretch for four miles.

The rocks are wonderful, superb natural archways and passages of great height, possibly unique in their way even here. Their beauty is wild and romantic and we lunched on a small plateau (as it were) commanding a view of all these wonders. We could see St Agnes Head and the Bowden Rocks on our left and on the right Penhele Point and the Gull Rocks could be seen. And it was in this direction that we wandered, coming at length to the great sand dunes where we had a stiff climb up the cliffs and went in search of the lost church St Piran in the Sands.

Legend declares that St Piran (patron saint of Tinners) built the church which was buried in a sandstorm which swept over the land. It was excavated in 1835 and has since been enclosed in a concrete outer building. We were fortunate in at once striking the right path and easily found the church which still lays in such a hollow that it cannot be seen till one is quite close.

Figure 62: *St Piran Church during building of 'Preserving Structure', 1910*

Our good fortune did not end here for the church was open. The vicar of Perranporth was conducting a friend over it (as he keeps the key) so we had the great privilege of entering the building. There is however little to see, the length of the building being only some thirty feet and the width about thirteen feet and the height also about thirteen feet. Part of an altar still remains and an old doorway (ninth century). We had a stiff walk over the sand dunes by the cliff path back to Perranporth but with lovely views of coast and country all around. A very enjoyable tea at the Red House (good) and we then walked to the station and the train being late, had a nice long time to admire the beautiful valley which seemed to gain greater charm in the light of the fast approaching sunset of a perfect day.

Tuesday

Lovely morning again, started early for our walk to Bedruthan Steps. We took the narrow road on the right of the church and after dropping quickly into the valley, we ascended the steep hill opposite from which we had a glorious view of the Porth and valley. The road is sweetly pretty, in many parts truly a country lane with trees meeting overhead and we followed this for some time till we came to Lower Trenance Farm, prettily situated among trees, quite an ideal restful spot, then up a long field to Upper Trenance, being escorted in this part of our way by two most charming little boys hailing from Tadworth and so prettily spoken. We left them as we entered the road again (here finding some luscious blackberries) and continued on our way to Mawgan Porth passing by 'Deer Park' and 'The Traveller's Rest' on higher ground once more. Then crossing the Porth and with a scramble over a hedge we struck a path on the cliffs and so reach the Bedruthan road. Here the road is a private one and we pass through several gates, the cliffs being here like a huge common, and we arrive at the Steps immediately.

There is only one building (tearoom) at the top of the cliff and the sight of the rocks is magnificent. The cliffs are precipitous and from the sandy beach rise huge rocks of peculiar shapes and forms. Queen Bess is one of the most noted. We descended the many steps which lead to the beach, and having lunched spent about two hours exploring. One realises how small we are among these towering giants and wonders and yet we are truly the greater miracles of God's hand.

We climbed again and had a delightful walk back, being especially pleased at finding several short cuts. The air was fresh and invigorating and renewed our energy. We gathered quite a lot of blackberries, having nice time to enjoy the walk itself and find new ways. Eventually we arrived back on the same road that we started. One of our most enjoyable days !!

Wednesday

Spent the whole day in the Porth having a real lazy time, bathing and climbing and especially exploring the bay on the left of Trevelgue Head – Whipsiderry.

It was lovely to have time to enjoy the beautiful sands. After tea at Mrs Roberts' Tea Rooms we returned to Cross Mount where we rested till dinner, after which we walked again to the headland but it was so dark and weird that we could not venture as far as we intended.

Thursday

A very wet morning which was disappointing as we had booked seats in the motor charabanc to Tintagel. We started however, well-prepared and with hopes of the sunshine triumphing which hopes were fulfilled. We passed en route St Columb Major, a quaint old-fashioned village comprised mainly of one long street, very steep, on the top of which is the church; the Nine Maidens, tall upright stones of unknown origin on the main road; and then on to Wadebridge getting some fine extensive views of the country.

Just before descending into Wadebridge there is a charming view of the coast with Padstow in the near distance and the River Camel which, with the woods above the town, greatly adds to the beauty. We cross the old 15th century bridge (probably the finest of its kind) and climb again at once. From here to Camelford the scenery is charming and extensive, the hills and valleys are verdant in contrast to the barer scenery of the coast of which we here and there obtained a glimpse.

We skirted Camelford and made for Tintagel. For some distance before entering the valley the scenery is wilder and grander and the rocks rise high on either side and we enter, as it were, a gateway of these rocks to the grandeur, each moment revealing itself. We arrived in a very heavy mist (which greatly added to the wildness of the place) but by the time we alighted this had given place to glorious sunshine.

We proceeded on foot past the Old Post Office to the bay and climbed up the ruins of King Arthur's Castle. Only a few of the old walls remain, but the views obtained are superb while in the immediate vicinity are sheer like cliffs rising to a great height. The whole combines to create a never-to-be-forgotten impression. We took car to Boscastle, had a delightful run and obtained good views of the coast all the way. The approach to Boscastle simply charmed us, dropping down into the lovely Valency Valley in which the town is built.

Figure 63: *Tintagel*

We walked to the little natural harbour which is shut right in from the sea and climbed onto the headland from which again we had glorious views of the magnificent coast and also of a wide stretch of country, the island of Meachard being directly below.

Figure 64: *St Symphorian, Forrabury*

We wended our way from this point over the fields to Forrabury Church, dedicated to St Symphorian, but which had recently been renovated, very much spoiling it. The old pulpit and oak bench ends, which latter now form the altar, being the only old parts left. Noting the old cross on the road outside the church, we descended once more into the village and having had tea remounted our car for the homeward journey, the beginning of which was indeed most lovely for we immediately ascended the hill out of the beautiful valley. And as we wound round had most lovely views of Boscastle nestling among the trees and sheltered by the headlands and cliffs, on the top of which the cultivated country could be seen for miles, and the sheaves of corn ready for carting added considerably to the picturesqueness of what will live in our memories as one of the most lovely of these Cornish scenes (I had pictured Boscastle so bleak and bare!). After this we returned the same way we had come, glad to confirm in the lovely sunshine the impression of the beautiful and extensive scenery.

Friday

Spent the whole morning on the Trevelgue headland, found a very comfortable spot with a delightful view of the coast to Trevose Head. After lunch walked over the fields to Crantock, passing on our way Edgecombe Avenue, with its charmingly pretty homes, and the public pleasure grounds which were very gay with lovely flowers. These were situated under the Trenance viaduct and one gets a charming picture when entering Newquay in the train. We were able to cross the Gannel by the plank bridge as the tide was out and made our way along the sands to Penpol Creek and ascended a very steep but pretty road to Crantock. We found it to be a very small village with a few old-fashioned houses as well as some newer ones. The village contains an old well, over which a stone mound has been built, but the place of interest is the church dedicated to St. Carantoc, considered to be the finest in the north of Cornwall.

It is very beautiful and extremely interesting, contains work of the thirteenth, fourteenth, fifteenth and seventeenth centuries, the font being dated 1474. There is a particularly fine screen (fairly recent) and some fine stained glass windows. The recent restoration is entirely in harmony with the spirit of the building. The fast approaching sunset made beautiful our homeward way.

Saturday

A very lazy day in the Porth. Called to see Mrs Roberts at the Tea Rooms and had a look round her little shop and bakehouse. We then made for the headland and spent an enjoyable morning. After our sandwich lunch we went down into Whipsiderry Bay and bathed. After tea at the tea house we had a delightful walk over the cliffs to Watergate Bay, the gorse and heather on the cliffs make a sweet picture. We returned along the sands, having a fine view of the cliffs. The colourings were beautiful in the sunshine and we stayed many times to watch the lovely effect and to examine the caves and the ferns which grow on the walls. After a scramble among the rocks trying to find the Banqueting Hall Cave we climbed the cliff and returned home to dinner, after which we took a short stroll around the village.

Sunday

Had a very nice morning on the headland, the afternoon we spent in the fields and in the evening walked to the Wesleyan Chapel in Newquay. A very nice day indeed.

Monday

This morning we bade our farewell to the Porth, this time being successful in finding the Banqueting Hall. We called and said goodbye to Mrs Roberts, whom we both like very much, and returned to lunch and then drove into Newquay, having a most comfortable journey back to London and enjoying all the beautiful scenery en route.

Figure 65: *Banqueting Hall Cave*

How nice to be home again after it all, yet how enjoyable it all was! And how thankful we are to God for his blessings and inspirations!

8.

August 1916
North Cornwall (Bude)

Saturday, August 12th

With Eva, entrained at Waterloo for Bude, passing through familiar country till we reached Okehampton, which town and surroundings are exceedingly pretty, the railway station being built on the downs and commanding a fine view of the town which lies in a wooded valley beneath. From here we travel over downs clad in gorse and heather, while here and there are beautiful valleys with running streams and tree-clad hills. After passing Holsworthy, a fair-sized place, we soon reach Bude and our destination, Rose Cottage, King Street (Mrs Abbott).

Bude is a charming old-fashioned town, the houses are very quaint and built in irregular order, though some good terraces are springing up. It is built in a crescent with almost an island in the centre. The Bude and Holsworthy Canal runs on one side and the River Strat on the other, the latter crossed by two bridges, one a wooden structure called Nanny Moore's Bridge and the other of stone. Here stands the castle, a charming place at the mouth of the river and surrounded by lovely greenswards: beyond lies Bude Haven, opening to the sea and the sands and cliffs. The coast is grand and huge rocks lie on the big stretch of sands which extend for 3 miles or more.

Sunday

A charming walk by the sea is by crossing the downs, which are but a few yards from our little street. A ten minute walk brings us on to the Summerleaze Downs and the cliff's edge. A quiet morning enjoying the invigorating breezes and beauties around.

Figure 66: *Maer Beach, Bude*

We went onto the sands (by the part called Maer Lake), which are firm and dry and said to be among the finest on the coast. The cliffs are grand with distinctive markings and colourings of the strata. Spent the afternoon on the Downs and attended evening service at the Wesleyan Chapel, Revd Perry Gill preaching on *Fight the good fight of faith, lay hold on eternal life*. After service we crossed the canal and over the cliff to the breakwater, which is a structure of irregular stones. At the left are piles of huge rocks, above which rise the cliffs of Compass Hill. Returning we climbed the latter, gaining a grand and extensive view of the coast. On our left Trevose Head with its lighthouse, Pentire Point,

Tintagel, Boscastle, Crackington Haven, Millook, Widemouth Bay and Efford Downs, and on our right Lundy Island, Morwenstow, Coombe, Sandy Mouth, Northcott Mouth. The thunder of the waves can be heard ten miles inland, a glorious sea this night.

Monday

The morning on Summerleaze Downs, grand sea, perfectly blue sky. After noon, a delightful walk over the Efford Downs to Widemouth Bay by way of Compass Hill and Efford Ditch.

Widemouth Bay is a quiet little spot of only a few houses and a very old cottage where we had tea. Here at this point the cliffs practically disappear, the land being nearly level with the beach. We did not walk the whole extent of the bay, but turned in to a field path for Helebridge, taking the canal path for Bude, on reaching which we saw the very finest of rainbows, a perfect and double one at both ends, its reflection being seen on the trees.

Tuesday

Spent the day on the downs wandering about as we felt inclined. At Menachurch Point we scrambled down the cliff to the beach and walked along the beautiful firm sands to Sandymouth (Eva would call it Sandy Cove). Huge cliffs towered above, their colourings shown up to perfection in the sunshine of a perfect summer day. Sandymouth is a sweet spot, a pretty valley with hills rising on either side. We hailed with delight the little tea house (just a caravan) and enjoyed the charming scene whilst partaking of it. We returned home over the cliffs and after our evening meal watched a grand sea from the breakwater.

Wednesday

Bathed and wandered amongst the rocks on the sands in the bay just beyond Maer Lake. In the evening took our usual walk to the breakwater, the sea more calm but a grand sunset.

Thursday

The morning on the downs and in the afternoon a pretty walk to Stratton by the field paths. This is one of the prettiest old-fashioned Cornish towns imaginable. It lies in a thickly wooded valley with tree-clad hills rising on either side. The streets are very quaint and narrow, and the houses very old. The most noted of the latter being the Tree Inn, formerly the Manor House of the Grenvilles. Here Sir Beville Grenville lived, who fought and won the Battle of Stamford Hill. There is an inscription on the outer wall to this effect. He had a body servant (seven feet four inches) who was born and died in this house, for whose coffin the floor had to be cut away to get it out.

Figure 67: *Inscription on wall of Tree Inn, Stratton*

The arches near the old Post Office, which lead to a courtyard paved with cobblestones, took our special fancy. The church has some good carving, the Jacobean pulpit is very handsome. In a side chapel lies the tomb of the Arundells of Trerice (we visited the Old Manor House at Trerice last year, seat of the Arundell family). Continuing our walk we took the Poughill road passing en route a field where the Battle of Stamford Hill was fought, a stone over an arch being erected to commemorate it. The view from this spot is very extensive and very beautiful. Poughill Church is very old and there are some fine frescoes and finely carved bench ends. A tablet is erected here to Goldsworthy Gurney, to whom there is also one at St Margaret's Westminster. The village is small but there is an abundance of foliage and the hedges are full of ferns. Returning to Bude we spent the remaining time by the sea.

Friday

We started in good time for our two days' tramp to Morwenstow and back. Our way lay by Summerleaze Downs, Sandy Mouth and Coombe Valley. Coombe is charmingly situated, it is a vast depression comprised of three distinct wooded valleys with a little stream running out to sea. We sat on the hill and enjoyed the beauty and peace of the place whilst lunching. Descending we come to the half dozen houses of which the village is made up, the principal one being the Mill House where good luncheons and teas are provided and where there is a most lovely garden.

Figure 68: *Mill House, Coombe*

Taking the cliff path, we had a very rough climb but passed through the loveliest of scenery – heather, gorse-covered hills, huge rocks and gigantic cliffs. No sound was to be heard but the shrieking of the gulls and the roaring of the sea, grand and awe-inspiring. After a long tramp up and down the cliffs we turned inland and quite unexpectedly came upon Tonacombe House, a beautiful old manor house of the fifteenth and sixteenth centuries and said to be the 'chapel' of Kingsley's *Westward Ho!*

Figure 69: *Tonacombe House*

Unfortunately it is not now open to the public. We followed a footpath at this point which led up through a thickly wooded valley, and a stiff climb on the other side brought us right into the garden of the quaint Old Bush Inn where we did justice to a good tea. No bed for us was to be had at the Bush Inn but we were recommended to Lower Cory a little further on, where we found a comfortable farmhouse (old-fashioned), with stone floors and wooden benches. We entered through the farmyard and the house was well away from the main road. After making sure of a home for the night, we explored the fields and woods around the house, which was quite near to the cliffs and commanded lovely sea views, with Lundy Island directly in front and away on our right Welcome House.

Saturday

We set out early to visit the noted Morwenstow Church where Parson R.S. Hawker worked for four years as vicar. After a short walk by field paths a grand sight opened unexpectedly before us, and across the valley we saw the charming and quaint vicarage built by Rev. Hawker. Its sloping valley to the sea, all gorse and heather clad, a scene now of peace and rest. The chimney stacks of the house represent the towers of Stratton, Whitstone and North Tamerton churches, two Oxford towers and his mother's tomb.

Figure 70: *Rev. R.S. Hawker*

The church dedicated to St Morwenna is very fine. A beautiful window is erected in memory of R. S. Hawker. In the churchyard many shipwrecked sailors are buried. The cliffs here are weird and wild, an ironbound coast with scenery of grandest description, its summits ablaze with furze and heather giving an impression of intense stillness and seclusion. With the Atlantic of the bluest colour and calm as a river it is hardly possible to imagine that it roars and thunders to the disaster of many ships. Descending the valley on our left we climbed to the coastguard station, which is built on a rock out to sea and affords fine prospects in all directions on the left Henna Cliff, rising to 450 feet.

Figure 71: *Hawker's Hut*

Retracing our steps to the high ground we found, after much searching, Hawker's Hut set in a secluded part of the cliff and built by himself out of fragments from shipwrecks picked up on the beach. Returning to the Bush Inn we took the main road to Coombe thence up a beautiful shady road, this the lovely woods of Coombe Valley and striking the cliff path, reached Sandy Cove where we stayed an hour or two. Then on to Bude, our outing finished but the memory to live long in our hearts, its beauty and peace to sink deep into our souls and give us renewed strength in the busy rush of life.

Sunday

A very quiet day. Went to the Wesleyan morning and evening, preacher Rev. Perry Gill (to tea with the Misses Hill). At night sat on the breakwater watching the sunset, getting a charming effect on our way home with the reflection in the canal. A very perfect and restful scene.

Monday

A perfect day with lovely blue sky. In the afternoon walked to Roddsbridge, and had tea at Wonnacott's Farm.

Tuesday

Spent the day at Widemouth Bay. Visited the tea rooms at the nice pavilion on the downs. Walked back in the evening over the cliffs, getting lovely effects in the fast disappearing light, Lundy Island and Trevose Head lighthouses being clearly visible.

Wednesday

Very wet morning spent on the cliffs watching a grand sea. In the evening enjoyed a nice little service in connection with the Children's Special Service Mission, which seems to be much appreciated. All the services are well attended.

Thursday

Lifeboat was launched in the afternoon. It was a pretty sight to see it attacking the waves and mounting them in so graceful a manner.

Friday

Our last day, and spent at Sandy Mouth, our favourite spot. We stayed long admiring the sea and the surrounding beauty, arriving back in Bude at quite a late hour.

Saturday

We reluctantly bade farewell to lovely Bude and the Cornish coast and moors, spending the weekend at Salisbury. We obtained comfortable rooms at 43 High Street, quite near to the Close Gate and many noted places of the city. Two doors on the right of 43 is the Mitre House, one of the oldest in the city. A short distance beyond is the Old George Inn, built in 1320.

A few yards down the opposite street is the old church house, whilst on our left the High Street gate to the Close.

We made at once for the Cathedral and were greatly impressed by the beauty and grace of the building and its exquisite spire, which seems to lose itself in the sky above. The stately elms with which the green is surrounded greatly enhance the loveliness of the spot. The interior of the cathedral is very fine. There are some beautiful monuments and windows and the carving in the choir is very lovely. The present building was finished in 1258, the foundation stone being laid in 1220. The cloisters, with the green and cedar trees, are said to rank as some of the finest in England. The chapter house was closed but we were able to catch a glimpse of some of the fine series of sculptures adorning the walls. The palace grounds are extensive, and so peaceful. We were only able to pass through a corner of them. The Close took our especial fancy and the old interesting houses were particularly charming (we had a vision in one of them which took us back to the days of Jane Austen).

The most noted houses in the Close are the King's House, The Deanery and Residentiary Canonry. The Bishop's Walk, with its fine avenue of trees leading to the palace, is on the eastern side. Some charming views of the cathedral are obtained at various points on the outskirts of the city, especially with the river flowing in front of it. Our most perfect view was after a glorious sunset, the glow shining on the West Front and the spire catching the dying rays of the sun. There are a large number of picturesque old houses in various parts of the city and all appear in such splendid preservation.

Figure 72: *Poultry Cross, Salisbury*

One fine specimen is at the corner of Silver Street opposite the old Poultry Cross, the latter being restored in 1711 and again in the nineteenth century. In the Market Place are some gabled houses, the Square being bounded by Ox Row, Oatmeal Row, Blue Boar Row and Queen Street. The Council Chamber was built in 1788. There is the old King's Arms Inn near the St Ann's Gate of the Close. The River Avon, which runs through the city, adds greatly to its beauty.

On Sunday evening we visited the church at Bemerton, where George Herbert lived and ministered 1630–33. A lovely quiet and peaceful spot. The church itself is very, very small. The vicarage just opposite.

Monday morning we returned to town.

9.

August 1917
Seventeen days in South Devon

Saturday

On August 11th Sis and I left by the 8.50am from Waterloo for Branscombe, via Seaton. From Seaton we had a pretty drive of five miles to the charming little village of Branscombe, obtaining splendid views of the coast en route.

Figure 73: *Farrant Hayes, Branscombe*

'Farrant Hayes', our home for two weeks, is situated in the centre of this very scattered village and directly opposite its only inn, the Mason's Arms. We found our rooms very comfortable, large and airy. After a welcome tea we started exploring. Our way to the sea lay through charming meadows, by running streams, a distance of ten minutes. The hills, with their green swards, rise on either side to a great height. The only house by the sea is the coastguards' cottages, now the property of Lady Lloyd as a country house.

Seaside Farm (where Hettie stayed) lay a little inland on the cliff. The beach is pebble and the sea dashes with such force that there are three or four strong ridges along the beach of quite a good depth. A few fishing vessels lay scattered on the beach completing a pretty picture. On the left rise white cliffs and Beer Head, and on the right red cliffs and Sidmouth. This contrast of colour is very charming.

Sunday

Branscombe is situated in the hollow of three beautifully wooded combes, the houses are built in clusters along its principal road which runs through the valley. Other roads lead off here and there to the summit of the hills and to the many farmhouses which lie scattered in the valleys. Many good footpaths lead through charming woods, where are to be seen in profusion beautiful specimens of ferns. Its situation is exquisite and one can obtain from various points many and varied views of the hills around. The cottages are charming, particularly that owned by an artist who has done everything possible to make it picturesque, the whole front being covered with rose trees.

The church lies high up the village and is of great age. Here we enjoyed a simple morning service and afterwards, continuing up the valley, we came to Street.

Our afternoon was spent on the beach and in the evening attended the service at the Congregational Church, Beer. Climbing the hill by Seaside Farm we came to South Down where one obtains a grand view of the valley and coast. On our left could be seen Portland Bill and on the right Start Point beyond Dartmouth. We had a lovely walk over the common to the charming fishing village of Beer, built in a narrow glen, a little stream running down its only street into the sea.

Figure 74: *Beer, Devon*

The bay is very tiny, rather cramped, its cliffs are white chalk. We felt it was rather spoilt by having many modern ideas introduced. Returning we took the cliff path as far as the lookout on Beer Head, then the common and South Down to Branscombe. Before descending into the valley we stayed to admire the charming view of Branscombe lying so peacefully in its pretty valley, giving one an impression of perfect rest and peace.

Monday

We spent the day on the beach, sharing it with about two other people.

It is possible to walk by the beach from Beer Head right away to Sidmouth, but being pebble is consequently very difficult. Folk do not therefore avail themselves of such a walk which would otherwise be very delightful. During the afternoon we clambered up the cliff, joining the landslip path and climbed onto the rocks of Beer Head, a delightful position for a grand sea view and a good blow.

Tuesday

We walked into Seaton after lunch. From Beer we took the path which leads onto the top of the cliff, a very lovely walk. Before descending into Seaton we obtained a very fine and extensive view. On the opposite side of Seaton runs the River Axe and below the hills which separate Seaton from Lyme Regis nestles the little village of Axmouth. After tea in Seaton we returned via the downs to Branscombe.

Wednesday

Taking the field path from the churchyard we came to a lane leading through beautiful woods, the hedges covered with lovely ferns. After a very stiff climb we gained the top of the cliff and here rested a while to regain our strength and enjoy the wonderful view. On the summit of these hills there is said to be an old Roman camp, but although we were uncertain as to its position we most probably passed through it. After a long and delightful walk with an invigorating and breezy blow over the downs we came to Weston Mouth.

Figure 75: *Salcombe Regis*

This little inlet to the sea has one beautiful wooded combe with running stream. There are only four cottages on the beach, which were once occupied by the coastguards. We had a very stiff descent down the cliff by a very bad path. Being unable to get tea at the cottages, we climbed the valley again, only this time on the other side. After passing through a farmyard at the top of the hill, we joined the road and in a few minutes came to Salcombe Regis. This village is comprised of half a dozen good houses with a church and several cottages. It is prettily situated some distance from the sea, but commands a very fine sea view. After tea our return walk was by the road and Littlecombe Hill to Street.

Thursday

Spent on the beach with tea at Seaside Farm.

Friday

Had a very windy walk over the Common to Beer, bringing Hettie and Gertie back to a charming tea at Farrant Hayes. After tea we walked by the landslip path to Beer Head, then climbing the cliff to the lookout and returning our usual way.

Saturday

After bathing we took a long walk along the beach nearly to Weston Mouth. Climbing the cliffs, which are a very great height, we obtained some fine views. Tea at Weston Farm, returning by road.

Sunday

Attended services at the Wesleyan. After evening service we climbed up the hills by the path opposite the chapel. Here we sat on the cliff for some long time watching the sun gradually sink behind the hills. A beautiful sunset and wonderful view seen in the light of the setting sun. The daylight had gone ere we reached the valley by way of the coastguard's cottage.

Monday

A superb morning with the sea a most perfect blue, we chartered our gallant steed for a drive into Seaton, having however to walk the first 1½ miles uphill to gain the level of the Beer Road. The beautiful colourings of the cliffs, sea and country looked perfectly lovely in the golden sunshine of a summer day. At Seaton, crossing the River Axe, we took the lane path leading to the golf links.

After a lovely blow over the cliff we reached the landslip path. Here, for about two miles, we walked through a maze of gorgeous colourings, sometimes under an arch of trees and sometimes a rocky mass, whilst everywhere was abundant with bracken and ferns and beautiful berries. We did not continue further than the cottage, but after resting a while by the edge of the sea retraced our steps back to Seaton, thence road to Beer and at the top of Beer Village we took a short cut through cornfields, reaching by the Beer Road just at the top of the village.

Tuesday

Started our tramp to Exmouth, taking the road from Branscombe to Salcombe Regis, about 2½ miles. From this point we passed over the Salcombe Downs to Salcombe Hill. These Downs rise 500 feet above sea level and are gaily coloured with lovely heather. We obtained very fine and extensive views of the country and coast. Salcombe Hill, which runs through woods, is a long, steep descent into Sidmouth. The trees on either side making a beautiful avenue, whilst here and there are rather charming views of the wooded valley of the Sid beneath.

Sidmouth is a very nice little town, placed in charming surroundings in a large bay amidst a wealth of trees whilst landwards rise a succession of hills. We stayed for a short rest on its breezy promenade, then passing on to the end of the esplanade we ascended Peak Hill and after a long and stiff climb we reached the summit, obtaining here one of the grandest and most extensive of views, said to rank as one of the finest in South Devon. We continued our walk over the Downs passing through more woods and slightly skirting the coast came, after a long walk, to

Ladram Bay. This is quite a unique little spot. A small approach leads to the little bay, which is of grand rock scenery, everywhere of red sandstone with the arch rock on the left side of the bay. From this point we soon reached Otterton, a pretty little village with a number of fine chestnut trees surrounding a green, whilst quite close is the old Priory, still in splendid preservation, and the church, recently rebuilt by Lady Rolle of Bicton House, nearby. Train to Exmouth, getting a good view of the River Otter en route.

Wednesday

By train to Tipton St John. On leaving the station we made our way to Harpford (passing en route the seat of Morrison Bell, MP, now prisoner of war in Germany) by Harpford Wood.

After about two miles we joined the main Exeter – Seaton road and soon came to Sidford, a little village two miles inland from Sidmouth, an interesting feature being its old Porch House where Charles II is said to have slept. After crossing the Sid at the bottom of the village we immediately started the ascent of Trow Hill, obtaining splendid views of the inward hills which lie around Sidmouth. The summit of Trow Hill is beautifully wooded and grand views are obtained from its summit. We joined the Salcombe Regis road and after making our way to Lower Weston Farm for a real Devon tea (not rationed), we reached Branscombe at 6 o'clock.

Thursday, Friday, spent in a lazy fashion on the beach at Branscombe. A very heavy sea, a grand sight watching the tremendous waves.

Saturday

Drove to Sidmouth and spent the day looking round the town.

We like the place immensely. It has a very nice esplanade, with Alma Bridge on the left below Salcombe Hill and on the other side Peak Hill. Below Peak Hill is the Royal Glen, where Queen Victoria lived, a charming old house bearing the coat of arms.

Figure 76: *Sidmouth Esplanade*

On the seafront is a splendid cricket, tennis and croquet lawn. There are some very charming and picturesque old houses below Peak Hill and situated high up on the cliff, which are now used as high class hotels, an ideal spot to spend a holiday. Beyond is the Coastguard Station, and one is able to climb to the top and so obtain a grand sea view.

The Church of St Nicholas contains some very fine stained glass windows, the west window being erected by Queen Victoria in memory of her father. The colourings are very beautiful.

After lunch at the Royal Hotel we spent some time on the Esplanade and afterwards left by the 5 o'clock train for Ottery St Mary.

Figure 77: *Royal Glen, where Queen Victoria stayed*

Sunday

The weekend proved to be a very wet one. We were therefore debarred the country tramp planned, but were able to get some walks by the Otter and a good look round the town with several visits to the church.

The church is indeed very beautiful, and stands on an eminence surrounded by some picturesque old houses, the principal one being the birthplace of the poet Samuel Taylor Coleridge, now the Rectory. The present residence of Lord Coleridge is a beautiful mansion, quite close. The church is said to rank next to the cathedral at Exeter and in some respects resembles it. The windows are very beautiful and the colourings and symmetry of the whole interior being in perfect harmony. There is a charming monument to Lady Coleridge, first wife of the late Lord Chief Justice of England, placed in the South Transept, which also contains a very old clock restored in 1907.

Figure 78: *Ottery St Mary Church*

We left Ottery by the 3.30pm train for Waterloo, after a delightful and perfectly happy time spent in the company of 'my friend Sis'.

10.

September 1919
Two weeks in Barmouth, North Wales

On September 6th, Edie, Sis and I travelled from Paddington, 10.15am for Barmouth via High Wycombe, Warwick, Leamington, Shrewsbury, Ruabon. At this point we passed through the beautiful valley of the Dee, then on to the charming town of Llangollen with its picturesque bridge and falls (the old bridge is said to be one of the seven wonders of Wales).

Figure 79: *Barmouth Bridge*

We had time to alight and get a good view of the town from the railway platform. It lies in a sheltered valley seven miles in length. We then passed on to Corwen and Bala, and the beautiful Bala Lake (largest in Wales being 4 miles long and ¾ wide) then on to Dolgelley and down the Afon Mawddach to Arthog, then over the Barmouth bridge which spans the estuary to Barmouth.

Barmouth is charmingly situated in Cardigan Bay at the mouth of the Mawddach. It is picturesquely surrounded by a range of hills, gorgeously coloured with heather and gorse. There are narrow winding paths which lead to the summit where some of the finest and most perfect views of Cardigan Bay are obtained. On a clear day can be seen Bardsey Island and the coast round Pwllheli and on the left Llwyngwril and the coast leading to Towyn, whilst inland one obtains a grand view of the Mawddach estuary and the Cader range.

On Sunday we attended the Wesleyan chapel morning and evening, and in the afternoon we climbed Barmouth Hill, 870ft, or Craig Abermaw, on which old Barmouth is built. We had a grand and clear view of the points just named. River, sea and mountain, covered in purple heather and emerald green fern, made a perfect picture indeed. In the evening the very fine male choir sang some of the grand old Methodist hymns and other items, a real inspiration.

Monday

We walked to the noted Panorama Walk, reached by taking a steep incline just above Barmouth Bridge. It is a charming walk, affording most magnificent views of the estuary and the hills on either side. We sat amid the heather, admiring the scene varied at every turn. After eating our lunch, we made our way high up the hills and had tea at a cottage overlooking Barmouth Bridge and the sea, then still climbing we had a rough but lovely walk over the hills behind Barmouth. After wandering about for some time, we managed to strike the right path and descended into Barmouth by the road against the Parish Church.

Tuesday

The sands are very fine and hard and at low tide there is an expanse of ¾ of a mile in places. We walked along the sands for about four miles, passing Llanaber, then turned inland by crossing the railway at Tal-y-bont halt. Reached the village of Tal-y-bont, a mile from Dyffryn. Here the hills are some little distance inland, Diphwys rising in the foreground. Tal-y-bont is a pretty little place, with the Ysgethin running down to the river. We had a tea in a pretty garden adjoining a woollen factory situated by the river. A very nice walk home by the Harlech Road gave fresh views of the bay and hills gaily coloured in the light of the setting sun.

Wednesday

Sis' birthday. I woke up early and wished her many happy returns of the day and presented my *petit cadeau* with which she was very pleased.

Figure 80: *Coes Faen*

We hailed a boat at the harbour and after a row for about an hour landed on the other side and took the little miniature railway to Fairbourne. The situation is very pretty and the sands are lovely. We gained the Towyn road and walked to Llwyngwril. The road is built high up on the hills and skirts the coast. We obtained magnificent views of Barmouth and the coast. Llwyngril is quite a small village, the Afon Dyffryn which runs through is very charming seen from the bridge, being a series of falls over small rocks. Returning we took train to Barmouth Junction and walked over the bridge, passing Friars Island at the mouth of the estuary. Saw Coes Faen, the swiss chalet of the estuary.

Thursday

Figure 81: *Orielton Hall and Cader Idris*

A very hot day, 115 degrees in the sun. We had a very lazy time on the sands bathing, etc. and in the evening climbed Barmouth Hill. Everywhere was grandly lighted up with the approaching sunset.

After ascending by some steps to Barmouth Bridge we called at Orielton Hall (CHA qts) and went over the grounds, which are very pretty, affording very fine views all round. At 10 o'clock we walked to the bridge to see the highest tide of the year and the moon shining over Cader Idris was reflected in the water of the estuary. A beautiful but eerie sight.

Friday

A coach drive to Tyn-y-groes, leaving Barmouth by way of Porkington Terrace, and Aberamffra Hill, thence to the Dolgelley Road. The Cader Idris range and the estuary present a panorama of unrivalled loveliness, the road turning sharply to the right and then to the left, whilst here and there we pass some charming houses nestling amongst the trees high up on the hills. On our right, beside the river, our little swiss chalet Coes Faen, and on the left Caer Deon where Darwin lived.

On reaching the Halfway House at Bont-ddu we visited a waterfall, then continuing we passed Waterlow Hill, or Peace Plantation, planted to commemorate the Battle of Waterloo. Near here also are the St David's goldmines. We soon reached the road leading to Dolgelley, our route however is the Llanelltyd road for Tyn-y-groes. On the opposite side of the Mawddach is the noted precipice walk. On arriving at the Tyn-y-groes Hotel we made our way to the Rhairadr-du Falls (height about 50ft). They are very pretty but the most charming sight of all is the three mile walk by the Canlan Stream to the Pistyll-y-caen Falls.

The path which runs through the wooded valley of the Upper Mawddach lies high up on the hills, the Canlan rushes beneath and a range of hills rise on either side, beautifully clad with gorse and heather and a wealth of trees. The falls are 150ft high, and here are the Mount Morgan gold mines. The path still apparently leads indefinitely on this superb scenery and one's desire is to follow it. But we had to return by the same way, obtaining however varied views of the hills rising above the Afon Mawddach. There were crowds of blackberries but we could not stay to pick them. We took the same route for our homeward drive, obtaining here also varied views of the Mawddach and the Cader range.

Saturday

Figure 82: *Cors-y-Gedol Hall*

Had a flying 'lift' in a car to Llanaber and then walked to Tal-y-bont woods. After passing through the woods we crossed the hills to the foot of Diphwys. The hills at this point are very barren and wild, and the day being rather cold and cheerless accentuated their wildness. We branched off in the direction of Dyffryn, gaining a good view of the sandbanks of the Morfa Dyffryn. We passed through the farm buildings of the Cors-y-Gedol mansion and down the pretty avenue of lime trees nearly a mile long. Then after a splendid tea, for Dyffryn Station and took train to Barmouth.

Sunday

Spent a very quiet day and in the evening climbed on the rock (Barmouth Hill) to see the old part of Barmouth. The houses are built high up, one above the other, reached by steep stone steps, the ground floor of a house being level with the roof of the row beneath.

They are very quaint old places, built of grey stone, and not very inviting. We obtained very fine views of the harbour and Barmouth Bridge.

Monday

Took train for Criccieth, the line runs quite close to the sea and parallel with the main road. One therefore obtains a splendid idea of the country en route. We passed through Dyffryn, Llanbedr and on to Harlech. Harlech is built on a hill 200ft high, the castle stands on an imposing eminence. It is the property of Lord Harlech and is in very good preservation. From here we passed on to Penrhyndeudraeth and Portmadoc, which lies at the entrance of the valley of Madoc. We crossed the estuary by the railway bridge. Here one obtains a very fine view of the bay, whilst southwards are the Merionethshire mountains and the terminus of the Festiniog toy railway. After passing Wern we arrived at Criccieth.

We made our way at once to the castle grounds, where undoubtedly we had the very finest view possible. It commands an uninterrupted view seawards of the whole of Cardigan Bay on a clear day and inland of the town and surrounding country. We had an ideal day, which greatly enhanced the beauty of the place.

Criccieth has two distinct parades, east and west, with the castle in the centre. There are some very pretty houses and one or two hotels on the front but the George, which took our fancy, lies back from the sea on the main road. Seawards we had a splendid view of the bay and the mainland on the left, and on the right the peninsula and Bardsey Island, with Pwllheli in the bay.

Inland there is a magnificent view of the whole town and the mountains rising beyond Moel Ddu (1811ft) and The Rivals. We were able to pick out quite easily all the interesting spots and all the chapels, of which there are not a few.

Figure 83: *Lloyd George's House, Criccieth*

At the back of the town, on the rising ground, is the home of the Rt. Hon. Lloyd George. It stands in a grand position. After a closer observation we agreed that he had displayed excellent taste, both in the style of house and position and particularly the garden and there is a charming simplicity of an air of restfulness about it all. The Criccieth Green is very picturesque and has round it some very pretty houses.

On our return journey we boarded an observation car and were fortunate in obtaining from the Madoc Valley a magnificent view of Snowdon and whole of the Snowdon range. Altogether we had a delightful day spent amongst some of the many beauty spots which Wales possesses.

Tuesday

We took train to Arthog for our climb up Cader Idris. Soon after leaving the station we took a steep path for about a mile, then after crossing the old Towyn road we had a very stiff climb to Tyrrau Mawr, a plateau (2617ft).

Figure 84: *Cregennen Lake*

Grand scenes gradually opened out before us, the Cregennen Lake (800ft above sea level) looking very charming with its pretty little bungalow and boathouse, then on our right the Black Lake. The view from Tyddn-mawr is very fine and considered by some to excel that of Cader. After a rest and our lunch, we crossed the saddle (cyfrwy) and made our ascent to the summit of Cader (2927ft), called the Pen-y-gadair.

Here we were fortunate in getting a cup of tea, which we were longing for. We had an excellent day for our climb, perfect sunshine, with no clouds to mar the magnificent view.

We sat on the highest point and picked out, with the aid of our map, the various points – Llyn Cader lay at the foot and far beyond the estuary, the Snowdonian range. To the north-east, the valley of the Wnion from Dolgelley and the hills within a short distance of Shrewsbury, the south-west Dysynny Valley, the river running to Towyn. Every valley, river and hill was distinctly visible. After a rest we made our way to the Foxes path to Dolgelley for the descent.

Figure 85: *Foxes Path, Cader Idris*

We were unfortunately shown the wrong path and, although we had our guide which gave full directions, we were foolish enough to take the wrong path and for an hour had a very unhappy and dangerous time clambering over the rocks and loose boulders on the face of Cader. Divine guidance gave us instinct to make our way across the rocks rather than descend and we eventually gained the Foxes path. We had a rush to gain the Towyn road, where we obtained a welcome tea at Griffiths Pugh's farm (in October 1917 Mr Pugh gained the RHL Saving Medal and the Carnegie Medal for saving a lady on Cader, at great risk of his life). We were fortunate in getting the offer of a lift in a car to Dolgelley and just managed to catch the last train to Barmouth, feeling very tired. As we left Dolgelley it was getting dark, but on reaching Barmouth found it bathed in a glorious sunset.

Wednesday

Took the ferry over to the island and spent a lazy day watching the regatta from the harbour. There is a very fine view to be obtained here of Barmouth. We afterwards walked via Barmouth Bridge to Arthog and found this side of the estuary very pretty. Returning we had a grand picture of Coes-faen and the surrounding hills reflected in the estuary, whilst the colours of the gorse and heather on the hills above were thrown up in gorgeous splendour.

Thursday

Our first wet morning. After much deliberation we however decided to take the motor trip to Snowdon. The day was not good, but we nevertheless enjoyed our trip immensely. We took the Harlech road passing Llanaber, Tal-y-bont and the River Ysgethin, Llanbedr and the Nant Col, Llanfair to Harlech. Here the road is high, and on the return journey we obtained a very fine view right away to Pwllheli and Bardsey Island, crossing the Festiniog road we passed into Penrhyndeudraeth by a very steep hill. We then passed through a very pretty wooded road, ascended the valley and soon came to the Afon Glaslyn, and after crossing Pont Aberglaslyn where we joined the Criccieth-Portmadoc road we passed into the Aberglaslyn pass. The pass is very magnificent. It is bounded on either side by huge mountains covered with fir trees. Following the rushing Glaslyn we reached the Goat Hotel at Beddgelert. We had time to alight and visit the grave of Gelert. Continuing we passed through a lovely valley to Pen-y-gwryd, high mountains rising on either side and the Glaslyn dashing beneath. Before us the summit of Moel Siabod and on the left Aran, one of the peaks of Snowdon. In two miles we reached Llyn Dinas, a beautiful lake.

We passed up the valley of Gwynant until we reached Llyn Gwynant, which is indeed beautiful, and proceeded uphill for three miles, obtaining grand views of the lake and valley. The road is cut high up on the mountains and on looking back one gets very charming and varied views. We rise to 907ft and reach Pen-y-gwryd. At this junction we turn to the Pass of Llanberis and continue to rise for another mile and then start the descent of the Pass of Llanberis.

This is said to be the finest carriage mountain road in Wales. The noble mountains are very precipitous, huge boulders lie about in confusion and the river rushes to Llyn Peris. We passed through the pretty village of Nant Peris, once known as the old Llanberis. Here the country folk were celebrating their annual fair.

We passed on to the remains of Dolbadarn Castle and on the opposite side of the lake the slate quarries, then on to the foot of the Snowdon Mountain Railway. After a rest of one hour for lunch, during which time we saw the cattle fair, the auction being all done in Welsh, we continued to Carnarvon. We visited the castle, which is very fine, and the view obtained from the top of one of the turrets overlooking Anglesey is very pretty. From here we took the route via Waunfawr and Betws Garmon and Llyn Quellyn (1½ miles long) and then to Rhyd-Ddu and the Snowdon narrow gauge railway, passing the River Colwyn and in three miles reached Beddgelert, the return journey to Barmouth via the same road.

Friday we spent in Barmouth and at last found the cottage high on the rock in which Marianne Farningham lived. After dinner we spent at Arthog and, between the showers, saw a perfect rainbow shining onto the hills a perfect half-circle and a second one reflected. Quite the finest I have seen.

Saturday

We had to say farewell to Barmouth and all its glorious surroundings. We were privileged in seeing Cader and the range of mountains covered in snow. It was our last, and not the least, beautiful sight which our eyes had been feasting on for fourteen days. Our journey was very comfortable and we said farewell at Paddington after a very delightful time.

11.

September 1920
A holiday in Dunster, Somerset

Harry, Ada and Marjorie joined Sis and I for this holiday and we left Paddington at 9.30 having a splendid journey via Reading and Taunton, arriving at Dunster 2.30. The station is 10 minutes' walk from the town – 'an old-fashioned town in an old-fashioned street' – quaintly old world whichever way it is viewed. In the High Street is the old yarn market, erected 1609, which is in perfect harmony with the straggling old street paved with cobbled stones, on either side of which are very picturesque old houses. The Luttrell Arms, immediately on the left, is a very charming hotel and contains some splendid rooms with oak carving and oaken gabled roof.

In Church Street, which branches off on the right at the lower end of High Street, is a fine building known as The Nunnery. The Church at the top of West Street has a clock and chimes which play various tunes at 9, 1, 5 and 9 o'clock. The approach to our cottage is by a little stream down Water Lane, at the bottom of West Street.

Figure 86: *Dunster High Street with Luttrell Arms on left*

In front of the cottage a little brook babbles and a few yards on, beyond some charming cottages gay with flowers, this joins the stream over which a bridge leads on to the Deer Park. By this bridge we have our evening promenades. A noted meet of the staghounds had taken place in Dunster an hour or two before our arrival and we saw many of the huntsmen returning. On Saturday evening we had a charming walk into Minehead (three miles) by the upper road, which avoided motor traffic and afforded our first visions of sea and country in which we are to spend the next fortnight. Views on our right of Watchet and the Quantocks in the background, of the channel and the Welsh mountains in front of us, and on our left Minehead built on the steep North Hill, underneath which nestles the old Quay Town, quaint little fishermen's houses going back to the time when this was the principal industry. North Hill extends as far as Porlock Bay, four and a half miles from the Quay past Greenaleigh Point.

Sunday

Figure 87: *Grabhurst*

In the afternoon climbed a steep heathery ridge (761ft) Grabbist or Grabhurst by a road at the back of the chapel (Wesleyan). A very stiff climb up the face of the hill, but were well repaid by the vision of purple heather just at perfection and yellow gorse. At our feet on the left was the beautiful valley of the Avill, with villages of Timberscombe and Cutcombe and range upon range of hills beyond towards Dulverton. We took our tea and sat on the summit and before descending walked along the breezy heather-clad ridge. Beautiful weather and glorious views.

Monday

Walked to the Dunster beach, bathed and had a lazy time. After picnic lunch walked on beach by golf links to Minehead. Had tea at Beach Tea Rooms and returned by train. After dinner sat in Deer Park till bedtime.

Tuesday

Figure 88: *Dunkery Beacon*

Out very early to climb Dunkery Beacon 1707ft, and to catch the 8.15 bus to Wheddon Cross, but found the bus did not run on Tuesdays. Therefore took a by-road skirting Grabhurst through the Vale of Avill (Celtic Valley of Apples) to Wootton Courtenay. A lovely walk of about four miles on which we picked lots of blackberries. After lunch Sis and I climbed the Beacon and found it a very easy climb. We rose quickly and a splendid view opened out before us, enlarging as we ascended. Most of the slopes are clad in heather and give a beautiful purple effect. We gained the summit in about two hours and viewed the rolling sea of the hills of Exmoor, but a mist came suddenly up from the sea and we had to imagine the magnificence of the scene extending to the heights of Dartmoor and North Cornwall (fifteen counties can be seen on a clear day and a horizon of 500 miles in circuit is commanded). Returning, we descended by the motor road and were delighted with the beauty of the Exmoor scenery, with clear broad paths cut through the heather and the Horner Woods nestling in a combe to the left. We found we were on the path for Luccombe, so had to turn sharply to the right at 810ft and descend to Wootton Courtenay. We had tea in a garden and then walked home, same road.

Wednesday
Spent the morning on Dunster Beach and after lunch walked through the Deer Park, a part of the beautiful castle estate, to Carhampton, a small village with large orchards, in which were an abundance of lovely red apples, and so on to Blue Anchor.

A very pretty approach to this little place from the main road. It is situated at the water's edge with a new stone promenade, and when the tide is up one feels it is indeed the seaside with the water dashing with immense force over the wooden stakes, which act as a breakwater. Returned by last train to Dunster, 8.6.

Thursday
Motored to Porlock Weir from Minehead via Allerford and Porlock, obtaining fine views of the moorland and of the bay as we descended to the old fishing village. We went into the Old Ship Inn at the Weir, repaired but retaining much of its quaintness and charm. We then walked through Ashley Combe for 1½ miles, on a path high up by the edge of the sea, gaining views like cameos here and there of the glorious sea and beautiful cliffs (one of Countisbury Lighthouse) to our objective, Culbone Church – said to be the smallest complete Parish Church in England, and only reached by the sun's rays four months in the year. The church is still in use, but not nicely kept up. From here a path leads to Glenthorne, but we returned by the same route passing at the exit of the combe the summer seat of the Earl of Lovelace.

We then visited Porlock itself, a quaint old town with long, straggling, irregular streets and curious picturesque houses covered with flowers, creepers and fuchsias. We were fortunate in seeing the return of the hunt to this old world place, completing the atmosphere of the picture as they clattered through over the cobbled street to the Old Ship Inn at the junction of the Old Porlock Hill and the new Lynton Road. An old world appearance has this inn, and there is a fine chimneypiece in the room where Southey is said to have stayed on a rainy night during a tour in this part of the country.

Porlock   Coach at Ship Inn.

Figure 89: *The Old Ship Inn, Porlock*

The spell was broken by the modern touch of motor cars arriving for the huntsmen. We saw the dead stag brought in through the town – so small a creature for so many folks to hunt.

I should note that Porlock Weir is some mile and a half from Porlock and is reached by a steep and winding hill, descending which one has glorious views of the bay and hills around. The bay is said to be five miles across, from Hurlstone Point on the right to Gore Point on the left.

Friday

Morning in Dunster on the hills overlooking the sea. Early lunch and then rambled over Grabhurst by paths cut through the carpet of heather. Below were grand views of Minehead and the coast around Watchet. After descending from Grabhurst into Minehead, we had a stiff climb up the hill by the church steps.

The church is conspicuously situated high on the hill and is reached by steep steps, at foot of which cluster the quaintest of cottages. Magnificent views are obtained of the green country flanked by the Quantocks, with Dunster set down in the centre, the Conygar Tower being a very picturesque, prominent landmark. The North Hill has been described as the glory of Minehead, and we wound our way round the hill past beautiful houses set high up, commanding glorious sea views and views of the Welsh coast and of the town below, till we came at length – long length after enquiring of <u>every</u> person we met for the last mile – to Greenaleigh Farm where we had a tea, worth walking and waiting for.

Farm is built on edge of the sea, with the steep hill rising directly behind, and facing north gets the sun for but a few months in the year. We found a path through the pine woods which quickly led us to the quay and home by train.

Saturday

Figure 90: *Cleeve Abbey – view of cloister from Monks' Choir*

Morning on the beach and then took train after picnic lunch to Washford, from whence it is but a short walk to Cleeve Abbey. Founded in 1188, it was the residence of 28 monks. After the dissolution the church was razed to the ground and later the buildings were used as a farm. About fifty years ago, Mr Luttrell of Dunster Castle bought the property, had the buildings cleared away, and the place kept in a condition more befitting its ancient and religious character.

It is a fine old place, with a most charming maiden to act as guide. On a cycle of songs 'Songs of Old Cleeve' she is immortalised. We (Sis and I) then followed the path trodden by the monks on their way to Cleeve Church over the Monks' Steps – a succession of stones set in the pathway over the hill – and from the top of the hill there is a beautiful view of Blue Anchor and Dunster and on to Minehead. The church is interesting and in the churchyard is a fine cross, recently restored. We walked on into Blue Anchor and, meeting the rest of the party, returned by train to Dunster.

Sunday

A perfect day, grand sunshine, strolled down to the brook before breakfast. Afterwards walked through the castle grounds which are open on Sundays, having a closer view of the castle. We went to the Wesleyan Chapel, which is built on a Friends' burying ground. Had a picnic tea in the Deer Park. Walked to the beach in the evening – water very high, a glorious sunset, everywhere most lovely colourings. As the children threw stones into the water, there appeared to shoot up, as it were, rainbow jets of fire as the dying sun rays caught the spray. One of the finest days of the year.

Monday

Out early to catch the 8.15 bus to Wheddon Cross, which this time did not fail us, but was a ramshackle affair. Following a very pretty road we passed through the valley of Avill by Timberscombe and Cutcombe to the long ascent to Wheddon Cross (980ft), the largest inhabited village at so great a height in the country. Turning sharply to the right at the Inn, we found it but a short walk to Dunkery Gate. A mist was passing over and we waited a while, but as this did not altogether clear we crossed over by the coach road (1600ft) regretfully leaving the summit (1707ft) on our left, dropping to Cloutsham and obtaining on the way wonderful and extensive views of hills and valleys clad in heather and firs – Porlock, Hurlstone Point, Cloutsham and Horner Woods and Dunkery itself, purple in its covering of heather.

Figure 91: *Cloutsham Farm*

We found a most beautiful road, from which we had a short, steep climb to Cloutsham Farm, a delightful house (recently built to replace the old farmhouse burnt down) with rooms panelled in oak and situated in a grand position by Cloutsham Ball. We crossed the Ball, a very large field noted as the scene of the first meet of the season of the staghounds in the second week in August. We soon descended through the glorious Horner Woods, the river noisily accompanying us, the hills on either side clothed to the summits with trees, till we reached Horner Mill where we had a welcome tea.

About ten minutes' walk through a lane and fields brought us to the Red Post, where we were fortunate in getting a seat on the bus, which however picked up many more travellers before reaching Minehead, many standing and sitting on the backs of the seats.

Tuesday

Had really lazy day on the beach at Dunster, getting the water for our tea at a picturesque farm, once an old manor house of Dunster (the house is now rented by a Mr. Ford and the farm buildings and cottage let separately).

Wednesday

A great day. Motor trip over Exmoor, a quick run to Porlock as on Thursday last, thence by the new private road to Lynton, the entrance by the Old Ship Inn. The road is built through Whitestone Park, and ascends easily in zig-zag fashion through wooded combes to the open moorland where we get in full beauty the vision of which we have had foretastes on our way up. We now join the old Porlock Road at its highest point (1378ft) and then for some eight miles we are on the top of the moors, with a veritable sea of heather for many miles on our left – billows of hills, as it were, with lonely farmhouses, small villages and just beautiful wooded combes nestling away in the hollows quite out of sight.

We caught sight of Oare Church and the Badgworthy Valley, and on the coast side, Glenthorne, and so came to the County Gate where the 'Summershire' meets the cider country, and we enter Countisbury and descend one of the steepest hills in the country into beautiful Lynmouth, with its sister town keeping watch on the hill above. We gladly renewed our acquaintance made in 1914 with this lovely spot, ascending by the cliff railway to Lynton, visiting the North Walk and wonderful Valley of Rocks, and so through the town by the Castle Hotel back down to Lynmouth. After visiting Watersmeet we gradually climbed onto the moors again by Brendon Two Gates on to Simonsbath, the 'capital' of Exmoor. The approach to this miniature metropolis is by the descent of a long hill through cultivated land, high beech hedges bordering the roadway.

A church, a pretty vicarage, an inn and a few cottages comprise this 'capital' and we continue through leafy lanes on to Exford, where we strike again the open heath at Comer's Cross and wind up Winsford Hill to a height of 1405ft, from which we were able to see Dunkery, the Wellington Monument and the tors of Dartmoor. Descending again, we reach the beautiful Barle valley at Dulverton, the southern gate of Exmoor. We alighted for an hour in this most picturesque spot and then continued, passing Pixton Park, the seat of the Earl of Carnarvon, crossed Hele Bridge, and followed the verdant Exe Valley to Exton, and then joining the Quarme and later on the Avill, and so arriving back in Dunster, our quaint little town.

Thursday

Climbed Grabhurst and enjoyed a rest among the heather. After lunch, Sis and I gained the topmost peak of this lovely hill and then descended into Wootton Courtenay. A very windy walk, but we enjoyed it immensely. Had tea at the inn and returned through a heavy storm to Dunster, but the storm raced and passed us and we entered home in the light of a beautiful sunset.

Friday

Rather stormy day, spent in Minehead. Saw the lifeboat return in all its festive array, as it was Lifeboat Day. Stayed on pier all morning, for a quiet time. Had nice tea at the confectioner's in the Parade Avenue.

Saturday

Grand morning. Saw Ada, Harry and Marjorie off to London with much regret, and then took train to Minehead and bus to Allerford village and walked up a shady lane to Selworthy Green, around which are built in irregular fashion the pretty thatched cottages inhabited by the old pensioners of the Acland Estate.

Figure 92: *Selworthy Green*

Each has a nice garden, and tea is provided for visitors by the old folks on the lawns or under the gnarled trees. An ideally peaceful spot to spend the last days of life in. We visited the church and walked on the outskirts of Selworthy Woods, climbing on to the North Hill. Leaving Selworthy Beacon, the highest point of the hill (1014ft) to which we were quite near, behind us we had a delightful walk on the top of the hill for about two miles to the pine woods above Greenaleigh Farm, having en route grand views of sea and Welsh coast and on our right Dunkery and the hills and valleys around.

We had a steep, rough descent to Greenaleigh, where we enjoyed our tea and sea views at one and the same time. We then walked on beyond the farm and took a steep path up the cliff, during which a storm came up and we saw a magnificent rainbow which spanned the channel. We gained the path and had a long and delightful descent into Minehead, seeing many of the paths and places which had now become familiar, and the many splendid roads over the North Hill, which had been made by Mr. Luttrell and to whom the property belongs. Taking the higher road into Dunster we were soon home.

Sunday

Morning service at Wesleyan Chapel. Lady preacher. After dinner took the path over the brook, which leads through a gate opposite the Deer Park, and climbed through a beautiful pine wood with thick undergrowth of ferns and bracken on to Garlick Hill, a mass of heather and bracken and in all the beauty of their autumnal dress. The woods wound round the hills and appeared to go on indefinitely. We eventually made for the road and, at the end of a beautiful lane where blackberries were blacker and bigger and sweeter than we had yet seen, we came to the Timberscombe Road and a short walk brought us to Dunster.

Monday

After packing up our 'bundles', we went out to 'do' Dunster Castle grounds, which are indeed lovely. We went close up to the castle, but were not able to go in.

Saw a lemon tree growing on the south wall, with ripe fruit, green fruit and blossom all at the same time. Dating back to before William the Conqueror, when it was given to the De Mohuns, it is very historical place but has been kept in good repair and added to from time to time. A very fine tennis court is laid out on top of the keep, commanding magnificent views of sea and country.

After leaving the castle we had an opportunity of being shown over the Luttrell Arms, once the residence of the Abbotts of Cleeve. A charming old place, with beautiful old rooms with oaken beams and panels, furnished artistically and comfortably and yet conveying exactly the atmosphere of the place. A charming garden at the back commanded a wonderful view of the town and of the castle. After lunch, we bade farewell to Miss Long, catching the 2.30 to Paddington, having tea on the train and a comfortable journey. A glorious holiday to live long in memory.

12.

September 1921
A holiday on Dartmoor

Saturday

Figure 93: *Deller's Restaurant, Exeter*

Left Paddington on September 3rd by the 9.25am train for our holiday on Dartmoor. We had a comfortable run to Exeter, where we stayed 2½ hours. After an excellent lunch at Deller's, a picturesque restaurant in High Street quite near to the cathedral, we then spent three quarters of an hour in the cathedral, which we saw to the best advantage under the most favourable conditions, the sun streaming through the windows giving a rich mellowness to the beautiful pillar clusters. We specially noticed the women's window, erected by the women of Devon representing the various spheres of women's work, and the one erected in memory of Sir John Taylor Coleridge. The precincts of the cathedral looked very charming in the sunshine. The Guildhall in High Street, built in 1330, is a very old building and contains some fine pictures, one in particular by Lely of Henrietta, daughter of Charles I.

We much enjoyed the remainder of the journey, passing alongside the River Exe by the seafront to Dawlish and Teignmouth. The country from Totnes onto Ivybridge and Plymouth was particularly beautiful where we changed. We passed through the thickly wooded valley of Bickley, through charming woods and by running streams up to Yelverton, 700ft. There, we changed into a small train consisting of one coach and an engine.

Figure 94: *The approach to Princetown Station*

After passing Dousland station, the only station between Yelverton and Princetown, the train creeps in tortuous curves to a height of 1400ft. En route we obtain a fine view of Meavy Valley and church and the beautiful Burrator Reservoir, and wonderful views of moorland stretches of richly wooded valley. The moors as we near Princetown are very rugged and barren, with huge boulders scattered near the summit of the Tors. Our house is high on the moor on the Yelverton Road. Princetown, the headquarters of the Duchy, is the largest inhabited place on Dartmoor Forest and is situated on the Plymouth and Moretonhampstead road, just off that from Tavistock to Ashburton.

Sunday

Enjoyed a very nice bright service at the Wesleyan Chapel. In the afternoon took our tea on the moors and climbed North Hessary Tor, 1600ft, where we obtained a wonderful view.

The eye roves over miles and miles of moorland scenery surrounded by a ring of hills, beautifully coloured, it appears from the elevation like a tableland. Southwards the view extends to the Channel, inland the main roads over the moors can be seen for miles, some appearing to rise nearly to the summit of the tors until they are lost as they descend on the other side. The Burrator Reservoir appears quite near, Merrivale railway bridge and the Moretonhampstead and Tavistock and Yelverton roads are easily discerned. After evening service we walked up a wooded road by the chapel to Bachelor's Hall, by which runs the Devonport Leat.

Monday

Had a general look round the village and church and exterior of the prison buildings. In the churchyard is a memorial to three soldiers who lost their lives in a snowstorm on the moors near Devil's Bridge. The prison buildings and warders' quarters are very ugly grey buildings, many of the prisoners are out daily (Sunday excepted) working on the road or the moors or the prison farm. On the Tavistock Road, and belonging to the prison property, we found a delightful wood where we were glad to get shelter from the scorching sun. Through this wood runs the Devon Leat. At Rundleston we crossed North Hessary Tor into Princetown.

After lunch took the road to Bachelor's Hall and sat by a shady spot of the West Dart, where we stayed all the afternoon and had our tea. Later we had a delightful tramp over the moor for about two miles then, after joining a road, we came to a very charming glen by the West Dart with the hills gaily coloured with gorse. The road led us to Prince's Hall, said to be the Prince of Wales' house in this district. After walking through the pretty avenue of a quarter of a mile we joined the main road to Two Bridges, a delightful moorland walk in the light of the setting sun. At Two Bridges, the Moretonhampstead and Tavistock, Ashburton and Plymouth roads meet. The Two Bridges Hotel is situated in a pretty wooded glen of the West Dart, a picturesque bridge spans the Dart and the water rushes beneath over huge boulders. In 2½ miles we were in Princetown.

Figure 95: *Two Bridges*

Tuesday

Had a delightful walk on the Yelverton Road for about four miles with the moorland stretching on either side for miles. After passing under the railway bridge and leaving Walkhampton on our right, we took a path on the left and came by a charming typical Devon lane, with ferns in abundance, to the Burrator Reservoir constructed under the shadow of Sheep's Tor across the River Meavy. It lies in a very beautiful wooded valley and is a delightful spot in which to spend a day. We spent some long time in the woods, then crossed the bridge and in a mile reached Sheepstor village.

Figure 96: *Painting of Sir James Brooke, 1847 by Francis Grant*

After seeing the church, we found the grave of Sir James Brooke, Rajah of Sarawak, who lived at Burrator House, a noted personage in these parts. We enjoyed a very welcome tea in the garden of one of the cottages. The village is quite small but very pretty and charmingly situated in a beautiful valley. We made our return walk past the inn, and on the opposite side of the reservoir we had a lovely walk under shady trees but got hopelessly lost. Eventually we found the road and were guided to follow the Devon Leat back to Princetown. This we did quite well but got into a boggy part of the moor near Devil's Bridge. We however came out safely and took the moorland road from Devil's Bridge.

Wednesday

Princetown Fair Day. We spent the morning watching the sale of cattle and wild moorland ponies, all loose in the field, and were quite brave walking amongst them. In the afternoon we looked over the prison stables, which are splendidly kept, and later watching the prison sale of cattle which is a very noted one in these parts. Crowds of people came from a great distance. We afterwards patronised the sideshows and roundabouts at the fair, altogether it was quite a gay day for Princetown.

Thursday

Took an early train to Dousland station and walked to Yelverton, a place rapidly increasing in importance, and a fine healthy spot 700ft above sea level.

The houses are very pretty and are dotted about what appears to be a huge common but is really moorland and the nearest stretch of genuine moorland to Plymouth. The Rock is a conspicuous part of the common. There are many splendid roads over the moor, giving beautiful extensive views, one especially fine being near the station of the Meavy Valley and the village church. We spent some six hours lazing about under the shady trees and visited the church and Methodist chapel. Both are quite modern and very nice buildings. We were unable to get tea at Moor House. We were very charmed with the place, an ideal spot for a quiet holiday in a good centre. Later on our return, watched a grand sunset over the moors.

Friday

Took an early bus to Tavistock. The road passes over the moors via Rundlestone and the beautiful valley of Merrivale. After crossing the bridge over the River Walkham the road ascended very steeply under the shadow of the three Staple Tors. Within a mile of Tavistock the road descends into a pretty wooded valley where is situated this old-fashioned town. The church is very ancient and very interesting and in the churchyard are the remains of the old abbey. The Bedford Hotel, a picturesque building, was once the chapter house. Opposite is the market place, which had an excellent display of Devon produce, also the Guildhall.

Figure 97: *The Bedford Hotel, Tavistock*

These ancient buildings, clustered together by the River Meavy, give a charming impression to the visitor on entering the town. A path by the River Meavy leads to some public meadows where are excellent tennis courts and a cricket field. Returning we walked by the main road to Longford then took a side path over the downs. Here we eventually lost our way, but at Moortown, a very pretty spot situated in a charming valley, we were put on our right track and took the path over Vixen Tor, passing Windy Port, and after a delightful walk we reached the main road just above Merrivale. We enjoyed a welcome tea at the Post Office and a chat with the quaint old lady in charge and then trudged home by the main moorland road, and at Rundlestone crossed North Hessary Tor.

Saturday

After our strenuous time we spent a quiet day on the moor. It turned very cold and we had to seek sheltered places. In the afternoon discovered an excellent path, for these parts, a road by the 'Plume of Feathers' led us to a cluster of huge rocks where we had our picnic tea. Afterwards we joined the road on the moor to Peat Cot, a few white houses in a valley with the tiniest of Wesleyan chapels, a service to be held at 3.00 each Sunday only. Following the leat, which passes through Peat Cot, we walked back to Princetown.

Sunday

A dreary mist and rain all day. We could scarcely see beyond the garden gate. We enjoyed two nice services at the Wesleyan Chapel.

Monday

The mist cleared and we had a lovely day. In the morning we had a very nice walk. Taking the main road to Two Bridges we then followed the West Dart for some distance, the water rushing over huge boulders, the path leading through a thickly wooded glen, ferns growing in abundance. After about half a mile we came to one of several noted clapper bridges which were at one time the only means of crossing the rivers. The bridges are massive planks of stone supported by huge stone boulders. In the afternoon we had a delightful circular motor trip.

From Two Bridges, taking the Ashburton road, we came to Dartmeet. Here the East and West Dart meet in the loveliest of wooded valleys, with the water rushing over boulders. There is here also a very fine clapper bridge. There are several very pretty houses and a hotel. We continued our journey, climbing the very steep hill above Dartmeet, obtaining a very fine view of Hexworthy on our right. Passing through Ponsworthy, a hamlet on the West Webburn, we soon came to Widecombe on the Moor, noted by the song *Widecombe Fair*. It lies in a broad valley, the church has a particularly high tower. Outside the churchyard is the old schoolhouse, and two trees with circular resting stones. This, with a few cottages, comprises the village. We then passed through shady lanes to Buckland in the Moor.

Figure 98: *Clapper Bridge, Dartmeet*

Here lives Beatrice Chase, then onwards to Ashburton. The road led through delightful woods, majestic trees on sloping ground on our right into a deep valley, the ground covered with ferns, moss and golden leaves, and with the vivid green grass made one of the most gorgeous pictures one could ever wish to see.

Ashburton is a small town with very narrow streets. Tea at the Golden Eagle, and then we looked round the old Grammar School, church, etc. Resuming our journey, we made for Holne, passing through delightful country, a deep and thickly wooded valley with the rushing Dart beneath. This is said to be some of the grandest scenery of the Dart, and one can quite accept it. The picture of Holne Chase, set amongst this scenery, will long remain one's memory as one of the sweetest of pictures.

After crossing Holne Bridge, then a mile, we came to the village of Holne, charmingly situated. From the church is obtained a fine expansive view. The old-fashioned inn next to the church was once the church house, a very charming house. The church is an uncommon style. It contains a memorial window to Charles Kingsley, who was born at Holne Vicarage, and a memorial tablet to Leslie Pearce Gould, killed in France during the Great War, son of Sir Alfred Pearce Gould.

Leaving Holne village, we had a steep climb to Holne Common, which lies immediately behind the village, then a delightful run of three to four miles over the common with wonderful extensive moorland views, the common all gaily coloured with heather. We crossed Paignton Reservoir, a steep descent from Holne Common brought us to Forest Inn and the village of Hexworthy, a delightful spot but very isolated. In half a mile we reached the main moorland road just above Dartmeet, and then had a five mile run over the open moor to Princetown.

Tuesday

A wet day so could not go far, but managed to get nearly wet through in the afternoon by walking to Two Bridges and back. Had tea at Two Bridges Hotel.

Wednesday

Took a short stroll in the morning getting some very clear views of the tors. A wet afternoon and evening, so we stayed in and enjoyed a lovely peat fire.

Thursday

Another lovely day. We took an early country bus to Plymouth and had a delightful run. The views en route were delightful and very clear. We had a good view of Links Tor, with its church on the top. Passing through Yelverton we took the high road over the common, and gradually descended into Plymouth. The latter part of the journey was through the busy part of Plymouth and quite a contrast after the moors. We were favourably impressed with the place. There are some good shops and interesting buildings. The Guildhall is very fine and has some excellent stained glass windows. St Andrew's Church, close by, is very beautiful. The Hoe is delightful but artificial. The flower beds are magnificent and there are some interesting monuments, an especially nice one of Drake.

Figure 99: *Plymouth Guildhall*

We climbed the old Eddystone Lighthouse but it made us feel very giddy. Otherwise the views obtained are very fine. After enjoying the sea and our lunch, and picking out the many points of interest round the Sound, we went to find the stone on the Barbican to commemorate the sailing of the Pilgrim Fathers three hundred years ago for New England.

Figure 100: *Agnes Weston Home*

Figure 101: *Agnes Weston*

After a second lunch at Matthews we took a car to Fore Street and saw the Devonport Naval Dockyard. Just outside is the Agnes Weston Home, a very large building, and much appreciated by the men. We returned via car by a different route and had tea at Goodman's. After resting on the Hoe we returned to Princetown by our bus, obtaining grand views of a lovely sunset. Before dinner we climbed on Hessary Tor but were a little too late, the best of the colourings had gone. Later a short walk to see the moors flooded in moonlight.

Friday

Another lovely morning. We made the most of our last day and took a walk round North Hessary Tor to find the Merrivale Hut Circles and Rows. With very little difficulty we found them just off the Tavistock Road and close to the C. School.

The Rows are very fine and wonderfully distinct, the whole district is full of interest. There are two double rows, one 850ft and one 590ft in length. The form a perfect avenue.

After lunch we sat on the moors and in the evening had a run out to Postbridge on the GWR bus and saw another very fine clapper bridge, which spans the West Dart.

It is a pretty spot, with a cluster of cottages and a temperance hotel. We walked back on the main moorland road, scarcely a house to be seen anywhere. We were impressed with the magnificence of the expanse and the solitude of the Tors.

Saturday

A very wet day. We broke our journey at Newton Abbot, walked through the park and the principal streets of the town. It is a typical Devon town and in the market place there are some picturesque old places. We arrived at Paddington about 6 o'clock after spending a very lovely holiday.

13.
July and August 1923
Two weeks in Falmouth

Friday/Saturday
Travelled by 11pm train with Ada Stary, Marjorie and Professor, had a reserved carriage, arriving Falmouth 8.30. Found our rooms with Mrs. Hodges, 29 Trelawney Road, very clean and comfortable. Walk to beach and roamed about on sands. Very delightful front and beautiful sands. The old part of town is picturesque, quite a fishing place. Evening, Flushing.

Sunday

Figure 102: *Submarines on Falmouth Rocks*

Baptist chapel. Evening, Wesley chapel. Afternoon, walk on Castle Drive. Saw several submarines left on the rocks. After evening service a walk on the front, which is very delightful, gardens lovely.

Monday

Bathed. Tennis 10.30am. 2.30 boat to Helford River. Landed in little boats and spent an hour in the charming village of Helford. The scenery is more like Devon scenery, such lovely country lanes and an abundance of flowers.

Tuesday

On beach. Bathed. Afternoon charming country walk to Maenporth, a delightful little cove. Walked back by the cliffs, crossing golf links to Swanpool and on to Falmouth.

Wednesday

Figure 103: *St Anthony Lighthouse*

On beach until 11 o'clock, then tennis. Afternoon boat to St Anthony. Alighted in small boats at a charming little secluded cove for St Mawes. Had half an hour's walk to the lighthouse. We had an interesting time looking over it and beautiful views. Tea on the cliff overlooking Falmouth.

Thursday

Boat to Lizard, passing Manacles, Coverack, alighted at Church Cove, very wet. Walked up the charming little street to Lizard Church. Took photos, interesting old font. Grand walk to the Kynance Cove, but wet, wonderful coast views. Tea in a little fancy shop at the cove and walked back. Caught the boat at 5 o'clock, Falmouth at 6.30.

Friday

Wet. Went into the library and did some shopping. Afternoon stayed in, and in the evening walked round Pendennis, saw the submarines.

Saturday

Bathed and sat on beach. Afternoon boat to Flushing Regatta. Walked to Mylor Creek and had a picnic tea.

Sunday

Wesley chapel. Took tea on the rocks under Pendennis. Stayed until 8 o'clock. The men went to chapel. I called at Budock and met the others on the sea front.

Monday

Delightful day. Took boat to Percuil then walked about two miles to Portscatho, a delightful Cornish fishing village in the channel. Sat on the cliff for our dinner overlooking Gull Rock.

Drove back by the Portscatho Express to the boat to Falmouth. At 9.30pm on front, full moon, delightful and never to be forgotten sight. The lights of St Anthony and the rays of the moon shining on the sea.

Figure 104: *The "Porthscatho Express"*

Tuesday

Truro by bus. Beautiful scenery through Penrhyn. Cathedral. Back down the Fal. Beautiful scenery. After dinner to hear band in Queen Mary's Gardens. Another lovely moonlight night.

Wednesday

On beach. Bathed. Afternoon watched regatta sports. Tea at Swanpool. 7.30 home. Cards.

Thursday

Motor to Newquay. Lunch on headland then walk on beach. Home 6.30. Walk to sea front.

Friday

Bathed. Sat on beach. Coffee. Afternoon Pendennis Castle. Grand views.

Returned to town 6.55pm. Comfortable journey, very tired. Thus ended a grand holiday, jolly company and excellent in every way.

14.

February 1925
Trip to the Riviera (Nice)

Saturday and Sunday

Left Victoria 11am Feb 21st 1925. Arrived Paris 9pm. Left for Riviera 9.15pm. At daybreak we were nearing Avignon, which is a very ancient city. As the day wore on, the sunshine became brilliant and at Marseilles we saw the start of the Riviera under excellent conditions. From this point to our destination it was a journey full of interest.

We continued by the sea to St Raphael, passing enchanting coastal scenery, fascinating little isles dotted about in the sea and beautiful coast bays and inlets, whilst everywhere a lovely fresh green of new foliage, almond blossom and an abundance of mimosa trees, oranges and tangerines hanging thickly on the trees. At St Raphael we leave the sea coast and pass through beautiful country to La Bocca, where we again join the coast, then more delightful scenery to Cannes, passing just above the Golden Corniche Road which, like the train, winds round and round the cliff, keeping close to the sea, passing charming villas with beautiful gardens, all gay with flowers and floral trees.

Here at Cannes are seen the Iles of Lerins, which can be visited from this point. Just a little farther on Juan les Pins, with its beautiful sandy beach, then we come to Antibes and Cagnes, reaching Nice at 2.30pm and the Hotel Windsor a few minutes later, which is near the sea and Cook's office. Later in the afternoon we went for a stroll along the Promenade des Anglais, a three mile promenade, the sea a deep blue. Here there are a great number of magnificent hotels. Near the Getty Casino are the Massena Gardens, where there is a monument to commemorate the uniting of Nice to France.

Figure 105: *Casino, Nice*

Beautiful beds of flowers and palms adorn the gardens. On the outskirts of the gardens are very exclusive shops of all descriptions to the right of the casino, and the casino square where the open-air dancing takes place during the carnivals. Passing the English Church in time for evensong, we went into the service. It is a large church and has a large burial ground attached.

Monday

Visited the flower, fruit and fish markets, where there is great animation, then after walking round the shopping centre took a walk on the sea front and watched the French ladies promenading in gorgeous clothes. These ladies are fascinating but very artificial.

Figure 106: *Russian Orthodox Church, Cannes*

After lunch went by motor to Cannes via the Promenade des Anglais. At the racecourse we crossed the River Var, once the boundary dividing Nice from France, then passing by the ancient chateau (1320) which once belonged to the reigning monarch of Monaco, and still keeping by the coast we come to Cagnes and Antibes. Not a pretty run until we reach the outskirts of Cannes. From this point we get a beautiful run, passing very elaborate villas with lovely gardens and a very peculiar Russian church.

Cannes is a delightful place with an extensive bay and promenade. We had a lovely tea, had not much time to see the town.

Tuesday

Great carnival starting at 2pm. We however took a trip to Monte Carlo, the principality of Monaco. After crossing the Paillon and passing the harbour, we join the Petit Corniche, a road built close to the sea.

We soon come to Villefranche-sur-mer, a charming place famed for its olive groves and beautiful villas. Its port is one of the best shelters for the French fleet.

On the Cap Ferrat is the villa where lives the Duke of Connaught. From this promontory is obtained one of the most magnificent views of the Mediterranean. In the next bay is situated Beaulieu, another delightful place, called sometimes 'Little Africa'. Then we came to Cap d'Ail and so to Monaco and Monte Carlo, a magnificent run.

Monaco is also on a promontory, but with many regrets we did not have time to visit it. Monte Carlo is a gorgeous place, the whole atmosphere is teeming with wealth, beautiful gardens, gorgeous flowers and hotels and villas, elaborate dresses and cars etc., all give one the impression of a place of frivolity, gambling and pleasure.

We strolled round the gardens of the Hotel Metropole and spent a short time in the Casino, then had tea and a walk round the town. On our return the moon came up, giving a delightful picture with the many ships and yachts in the sea all brilliantly lighted. This is a superb run.

After dinner a very magnificent display of fireworks from the beach at Nice, followed by the burning of King Carnival XVII (15ft by 4ft) in Massena Place, a grotesque image of plaster.

Then the plaster confetti battle, which we did not see as it is very unpleasant. The town is magnificently illuminated especially round about the casino and Massena Square. The Avenue de la Victoire having an awning the whole length of illuminations.

Wednesday

A trip to Gorge de Loup, leaving Cook's office at 10am via Promenade des Anglais. At Cagnes we leave the coast and turning to the right, steadily rise to Vence (1000ft), an ancient city with remains of Roman fortifications. Its streets are very quaint and narrow. We visited the potteries, which is the principal industry of the city. Cathedral is 13th century.

Figure 107: *Vence*

In the distance could be seen, perched high up on a mountain, the city of St Paul, 10th century, fortifications 12th century, invaded many times. Continuing to rise and passing many olive trees, a great industry in these parts, we came through beautiful scenery and splendid views of the Valley of the Var to Pont du Loup.

Its viaduct, which spans the Loup, is 200 metres long and 52 metres high. We lunched, which included the famous trout of this district. Following the stream and still climbing we reach the famous Gorge du Loup. The road winds round, bounded by mountains rising sheer from the narrow valley and overlooking the Loup. It gradually becomes more steep and after many sharp turns we reach Gourdon, 2200ft, a small ancient village with a chateau in which lives Miss Norris, an American writer who has bought and restored the village. There is a tiny church. A grand and extensive panorama is obtained of the Esterel, Mediterranean and country for miles around.

Returning we descend this beautiful scenery to Grasse, or City of Flowers, passing through the pretty village Chateauneuf Pre du Lac.

Figure 108: *Pont du Loup Viaduct*

Grasse has a population of 20,000 inhabitants. On its outskirts are splendid villas. Rothschild owns the majority of the land and has a large house. The town is beautifully situated on the southern slope of Mount Rosasar, 1600ft, grand views are obtained. The perfumery factories are noted all over the world. There are also preserving fruit factories. Evening, casino at Nice.

Thursday

Morning spent by the sea. Afternoon watched the Battle of Flowers on the Promenade des Anglais. Some of the cars were very pretty, particularly one representing Spain, with a Spanish outrider, the carriage containing ladies and men in Spanish attire, gorgeously adorned with flowers, as were many others. The contingent of 150 Australian boys visiting Europe, and at this time in Nice, thoroughly enjoyed the pelting of flowers.

Friday

Took a drive round the town, starting from the Boulevard de Hugo, a splendid avenue bordered on either side with trees. Avenue de Victoire, Notre Dame, Casino to Place Garibaldi, the Italian quarter and one of the oldest parts of the town. It contains in the centre of the square the Garibaldi monument.

Figure 109: *Garibaldi Monument, Nice*

The drive up to the Chateau Rock is very pretty and a wonderful bird's-eye view is obtained of the town and surroundings. On the right are seen the Antibes and Esterel Isles, and on the left the harbour and Grand Corniche and underneath, the old town with its narrow streets. Then beyond the new town and farther away, the hills with fine villas and immense hotels, and then beyond the mountains and Alps which surround Nice.

Saturday

Shopping and walk on the seafront. 2.30pm started on our homeward journey, enjoying very much the delightful scenery along the Riviera to Marseilles. Second impressions were even finer than the first.

15.
Easter 1926
Trip to Holland

Thursday, 6.00, Victoria to Gravesend, Batavier steamer to Rotterdam, 13 hours.

Figure 110: *Batavier III*

8am Good Friday, Rotterdam. An old-fashioned, busy town with numerous quays and bridges. Fine statue of Erasmus. St Lawrence Church (Groote Kerk) 1447, which contains a large organ. Train to Amsterdam. Hotel Polen on the Rokin near the dam. Afternoon steamer from harbour to Zaandam on the Zaan, thirty minutes. Visited hut of Peter the Great, resided here 1697. In centre of village, statue to Peter the Great. Most of the village folk wear the wooden shoes.

Saturday

Amsterdam, situated on the bank of the Gulf of the Zuider Zee, is a very busy town. The Dam is a large open square, the centre of business life.

It contains the royal palace, 1648, has a high tower with clarion of bells, also the Neuwe Kerk, 1408, in which the present queen was crowned, 1898.

Kalverstraat, principal shopping centre at back of hotel. There are four main canals, circle within circle, many smaller ones, a town of water lanes with 320 bridges.

From station, ferry to Tolhuis, steam tram to Broek in Waterland, a pretty little village noted for its cleanliness, houses mostly of wood. To Edam, famous for its cheeses, Roman Catholic, House Boat to Volendam, noted for its picturesque costumes (the headdress tells one which town or province the women come from). Sitting on top and inside of house boats pulled by one man and pushed by another, men mostly fishermen, religion Roman Catholic. From harbour at Volendam by yacht across the Zuider Zee to Marken (Protestant). Water here very shallow.

Figure 111: *Marken Fisherman*

Mostly fishermen, all in picturesque costumes, children looking very charming, men in full black knickers. Steamer to Monnikendam, fishing and agricultural work. Church 1420, tower and clarion of bells. Steam tram to Amsterdam.

Sunday

Presbyterian church in the Begijnhof, a small square which contains also the Roman Catholic church. The Presbyterian church was once the chapel of the Nuns, given to the refugees during the Reformation.

Stained glass window placed here in 1909 to commemorate the sailing of the Pilgrim Fathers.

Rijksmuseum (National), pictures by Rembrandt, Franz Hals, Helst, etc. *Night Watch*, Rembrandt.

Vondelpark – public park.

Willemspark, at back of Rijksmuseum, now the residential quarter of the better class which once lived on the quay as 'gentlemen's quarters', now business premises. This part reminds one of The Mall in London.

Monday

Motor to Haarlem, very flat, uninteresting run. In Market Square, Haarlem, monument to Coster, said to have discovered the art of printing.

Groot Kerk, huge gothic building, 15th century. Stadhuis, picturesque old building. Meat Market, 1602. Bulb fields between Haarlem and Leiden, 10 miles of magnificent blossoms.

The Hague, approached through miles of woods. In The Plein, statue of William the Silent, commemorating the recovery of Dutch independence.

Tuesday

Hotel Zalm, very comfortable and our hotel garden separated from the royal gardens by brick wall. The town has very broad streets, very clean, and delightfully wooded.

Visited prison (Gevangenpoort). Cornelis de Witt imprisoned here 1672, statue close by. Terrible instruments of torture.

Binnenhof, large open court includes two houses of parliament. Gothic hall (Hall of the Knights) most ancient building in the city.

Museum, in the Mauritshuis, contains splendid collection of paintings. Rembrandt's *School of Anatomy*. Also paintings by Franz Hals, Jan Steen, etc.

Figure 112: *Hague Conference 1899*

Palace in the Wood. Short tram ride outside city. Hague conference held here 1899, a charming spot. Handsome rooms, Chinese and Japanese, etc. The conference room walls magnificently painted.

Afternoon, Scheveningen, most renowned watering place of Holland. Twenty minutes' tram ride from The Hague. Delightful sands, very long promenade. Visited fishermen's quarters near harbour. Very clean, waffles and cream at an open air café on the front.

Wednesday

To Delft, noted for its Delftware. Thirty minutes from Hague, tram ride. Market place contains Church, Nieuwe 1381. Tower 375ft, gothic. Contains memorial to Prince of Orange. Royal mausoleum 1609. Prinsenhof, now a museum, residence of William the Silent. Room in which he was killed. In Market Place, old town hall, also statue of Hugo Grotius, great advocate for peace.

Palace of Peace, erected for the international Court of Arbitration. Carnegie contributed £300,000. Stands on thirteen and a half acres, outskirts of The Hague. Gardens designed by an English lady, the best we saw in Holland. Gifts towards the decoration and furnishing from every nation. England gave stained glass windows, a magnificent palace intensely interesting.

Thursday

Walk round Binnenhof etc., very enjoyable. After early lunch, train to Rotterdam, steamer from quay to Dordrecht.

Hotel Bellevue on quay. Our room on the corner commands a magnificent view of the River Maas. Adjoining is an ancient city gate, 1618.

Figure 113: *Hotel Bellevue, Dordrecht*

Dordrecht is a place of great antiquity. The River Maas is very wide, town thoroughly Dutch in appearance. Very busy. A tremendous amount of traffic on the river and the quay. Quays planted with trees, windmills, dockyards, etc. abound everywhere.

Church gothic, 14th century, very beautiful, best we saw in Holland. Very large, being very thoroughly restored. Marble pulpit, fine brass screen, fine carved stalls, some very good family vaults.

Canals. The old part of the town round the principal canals very picturesque.

Museum. Ancient and modern paintings.

New part of town very nice. Wooded wide streets, public park, large houses and gardens.

Saturday

Steamer to Rotterdam. Jolly tea. Batavier steamer to Gravesend.

16.

August 1926
Wensleydale, Yorkshire

Aug 20
7.40pm dinner on train. York Station Hotel.

Aug 21
Breakfast with Mr and Mrs Dablo. York Minster and quaint streets. Reaching Askrigg, 'Friend' showed us way to Bainbridge. Invited to 'meeting'.

Aug 22
Quaker meeting morning. Wesleyan Askrigg evening.

Aug 23
Morning in fields. After Semerwater met Mr. Thorpe, 'Friend'.

Aug 24
Climbed Top Scar, sat all morning. Late afternoon went to Mill Gill Foss, Askrigg, Askrigg Common, 1600ft rising to 1800, above which then Whitfield Foss.

Aug 25
Afternoon walked to Nappa Hall, Woodhall, tea at cottage.

Aug 26

Figure 114: *The Old Hall, Askrigg*

Cheese factory across green. Harper Bainbridge. Afternoon Askrigg, tea at Old Hall.

Aug 27

Morning by river, by Yorescott Grammar School. Afternoon with Mr and Mrs Walker round Semerwater by way of Countersett (George Fox visited here many times). Carr End good house for visitors. Marsett, tea by Gill Foss. Rydaleside through the pinewoods, property of Rydale Williams, late MP for Middlesbrough. Crossed Park Scar Foss at top (Black Ash Foss at foot) then to Stalling Busk and Bainbridge. Delightful view of the Bain above Bainbridge.

Aug 28

Leyburn School sports, excursion train early morning. Shawl.

Aug 29

Morning fields, afternoon anniversary at Congregational. Evening on Roman encampment with Mr. T and Mr. W. Seven o'clock Dr. C. Morgan, wireless service from Wesleyan Chapel.

Aug 30

Figure 115: *Aysgarth Falls*

Morning fields, after, Aysgarth waterfall.

Church tea at Platt Farm, Thornton Rust, Dr Wood's house at end of village with lovely garden. Particular Baptist Church, Cubeck, Worton then up field through woods to field path above Bainbridge.

Aug 31

Motor to Hawes Show (cattle, etc.). Tea at Mrs. Fosters' (25th Anniversary Wedding). Nine dishes on table, all home made. Evening walk to Countersett, Semerwater. Evening, cards at Thorpes.

Sep 1

Stile, Hawes Road. After lunch walked to Wether Fell and Dodd Fell with Dickie. Mr. Thorpe and Mr. W returning over Wether Fell to Countersett. Evening, cards at Thorpes.

Sep 2

Wet, stayed in. Hawes afternoon shopping, and back. Cards at Thorpes. Excitement – hedgehog in garden.

Sep 3

Friday, walked towards Addleborough, grand views of Semerwater and valley. Glorious sunshine and beautiful colouring. 1.28 left Askrigg with many regrets and farewells. Tea at Northallerton, York 6pm, Station Hotel, stroll around city.

Sep 4

Walked round city walls, service at Minster. Looked round the city. 2pm for Kings Cross.

17.

July 1927
Sixteen days' tour in Switzerland

Saturday

Left Victoria 8.28am for Zermatt via Newhaven, Dieppe. Smooth crossing, pretty country from Dieppe to Paris. Arrived Paris 6pm. Dinner then a walk round, leaving Gare St Lazare 10.30pm via Vallorbe, alighting for breakfast on the station, continuing by Lake of Geneva (Castle of Chillon) to Visp. Lunch at a pretty open-air café just outside the station, thence by mountain railway to Zermatt, a glorious run, superb scenery, grand weather. Arrive Zermatt 1.30pm Sunday. Hotel de la Poste (only fair).

During afternoon and after a good wash, had a delightful tea in the garden of the Hotel Seiler. Cosmopolitan crowd, very good music indeed.

At 5.30 service at the beautiful little English Church. In graveyard, many buried who were killed whilst climbing the Alps, inscriptions round walls of church 'Oh ye ice and snow, Praise ye the Lord', 'Oh ye mountains and hills' etc., and others. The church situated in a delightful setting, River Visp (Viege) rushing through the valley from above Gorner Gorges, and right down to Visp, with series of falls.

Figure 116: *English Church, Zermatt*

Monday

Walked to Gorner Gorges through the little village of Zermatt, along by the Visp, so charming, the gorges are very beautiful. Glorious morning, view magnificent of valley, mountains with pine trees and snow-capped summits. Fine view of the Matterhorn, Dent Blanche, Les Mischabel glaciers and magnificent waterfalls. Returned through pine woods via Winkelmatten with church 1607. Tea at Hotel Seiler, looked round most interesting shops.

After dinner, a stroll up the one and only street, a cosmopolitan crowd indeed. Street thronged and shops also, which are open 8am to 10pm. No horses or motors except the hotel buses. This place is closed during winter, no trains from October to May. Not a winter sports centre, 300 inhabitants remain, all food obtained beforehand from Visp.

Figure 117: *Gorner Gorge*

Tuesday

Edelweiss Café, fine view of Zermatt. Continued up to Trift Hotel, 7870, lunch. A very steep gorge with rushing water, beautiful falls through a rugged valley. We climbed to about 7000ft, fine view of the Gabelhorn and Trift Glacier. Returned to Edelweiss Café for tea, which was much enjoyed, the while obtaining one of the most magnificent views imaginable of Zermatt. Returned past the Goat Hotel, saw a male and female ibex with young marmot. Evening promenade up the little street and shops.

Wednesday

Had a quiet day with Sis. Left the party to do climbing whilst we strolled about various parts, enjoying to the full the glorious scenery and Zermatt. Tea at Seiler's Hotel then looked round the shops. Evening, usual promenade.

Thursday

Another glorious morning, not a cloud, the Matterhorn perfectly wonderful. At 5am saw a lovely glow in the mountains, folks already up, a party on mules climbing Gornergrat. We rose with the lark at 6.30am. At 7.55 were on the train for Gornergrat whilst the others walked. Alighted at first stop, Riffelalp, just above the pines. Saw English church erected by the Bishop of Norwich and friends.

Figure 118: *Kulm Hotel, Gornergrat*

Glorious views, perfectly wonderful. Many lovely excursions start from here. Continued to Riffelberg, 429, very rugged, no trees but many beautiful flowers, gentians in abundance. Walked to Gornergrat, 10289, Lunch at Kulm Hotel, highest hotel in Europe.

Magnificent day, all peaks visible, one of the finest views in the world and we saw it at its best. Monte Rosa range, Caster and Pollux, Breighthorn and the fascinating Matterhorn, Dent Blanche, Rothorn, Weisshorn, and on the south the Mischabel. Through a telescope saw a number of huts belonging to the alpine climbers, not visible to the naked eye. The grottos and glaciers wonderful through the telescope, look like huge boulders of ice. Walked all the way down.

At Riffelberg had a <u>very</u> welcome tea. Terrifically hot, hottest day I have ever experienced, even in the shade could not take tea out of doors. Went into the hotel to get away from the sun. From here we went through beautiful pine woods, the whole descent perfectly wonderful, flowers in profusion, views magnificent of the Visp Valley.

Friday

Left Zermatt, train for Stalden, 2630, mule path to Saas Fee (4 hours), but so hot that we took 7 hours. Valley of the Fee to Saas Grund. There we had tea, then a very stiff climb of 800ft to Saas Fee, passing little shrines, the fourteen stages of the Cross, and at the top an open church and on the walls were limbs and various parts of the body hanging, made of clay. Do not know the reason for this. Saas Fee, 5900, very primitive, only means of transit is by mule from Stalden. Our luggage came by mule. The Glacier Fee is quite close, good view of it from bedroom. Here we are the other side of the Mischabels, Dom 4554, and Alphubel mountains.

Saturday

Very tired after our long walk. Wet morning, rested. Afternoon, looked round the shops of this very primitive little place. They seem to sell everything that one might require. All the folks are peasants, mostly working on the land, work very hard and goats by plenty. All the women attired in old-fashioned long skirts and wear large white aprons, very hard working. Saw a very young couple working on the land with their baby in a basket nearby. They carry huge bundles of hay on their heads, mules heavily laden. Choir practice at 5.30 in English Church.

Sunday

English Church 10.30 and 5.30. We quite enjoyed being in the choir. At 6.30 we saw a large party of alpine climbers arrive. Had a meal at our hotel, sang in the village, they had come over the Alps from Italy. Quite a lot of life in the little place.

Monday

Charming walk crossing the valley and the beautiful, rushing River Fee. We climbed Golden Alp to the 'viewpoint', magnificent yellow flowers, hence the name Golden Alp. Lunch in a spot above the snow. Long rest, magnificent views of the Bernese Oberland and the Breighthorn snow slopes. Descended in terrific heat to the Grand Hotel for tea. Sun blistered my arms.

Tuesday

9am left Saas Fee. Walked down to Saas Grund, then on to Stalden. Glorious views through the valley. Rushing river, beautiful falls, very hot. Took us from 9am to 3pm, supposed to take four hours. Was frightfully jagged at the finish. Very nice welcome tea at Stalden Station. Train to Visp, then to Brig, change to mountain railway and went up the glorious and noted Rhone Valley to Fiesch. Heat overpowering at Brig. As we ascended it became more comfortable. Interesting conversation in French with a Swiss. Magnificent scenery, huge open valley, perfectly wonderful. Fiesch is a very small place, so beautifully wooded, such lovely refreshing soft scenery after the rugged scenery of Saas Fee.

Wednesday

Very restful and quiet, we had a very lazy morning. Fearfully hot, we could not exist except in the shade by the River Rhone. After lunch continued train up the Rhone Valley to Gletsch, the junction of the Grimsel and Furka passes via the Furka Oberalp railway. Travelling by side of the Rhone, passing Munster where ox carts were being used for hay. A wide, open valley at this point, many farms about. Centre for winter sports, especially skiing.

From Oberwald a very stiff, steep climb to Gletsch, which consists of the Rhone Glacier, Hotel Seiler, Post Office and English Church.

Figure 119: *Gletsch and Rhone Glacier*

Walked to Rhone Glacier before dinner. After dinner, very cold. Sat by a huge log fire in lounge. Big party arrived late, Polytechnic, all Canadians. Beautiful hotel, wonderful pieces of old oak furniture, huge dining hall and old pewter. Roman Catholic Church on fourth floor of hotel, erected by Alex Seiler.

Thursday

There is not much to stay here for, all very rugged and barren. Would be rather depressing, especially with the glacier so close. Early morning saw about 50 goats running home to be fed just under our bedroom window. The road diverges at this point, one leading to the Furka Pass winding up and up. Far in the distance is the very fine Furka Hotel, the railway continues up this side to Andermatt. We took the other road, leading to Grimsel Pass via Postal Autobus. Tremendous climb, wonderful views but sorry to say I could not enjoy it as it seemed so terribly dangerous. A wonderful road has been made and the Postal bus has always the privilege of taking the inside of the road. At times it is not too wide, and one's heart stands still nearly at this tremendous height with a sheer drop when cars have to be passed. However, we reached the top in safety and stayed at the little house and stopping place on the top.

Figure 120: *View of Furka Pass from summit of Grimsel Pass*

Then, descending this very rugged wild mountainous scenery, we reached the old Grimsel Hospice, now a hotel. Two lakes are by its side. We continued to Handegg and had lunch. There is here a wonderful waterfall on the River Aare. A big scheme is being carried out here for the supply of electric power for Meiringen. Here we continued for about ten miles through beautifully wooded soft scenery to Meiringen, passing Guttannen, Innertkirchen, very charming. On the other end of the gorge of the Aare, wound round the mountain and had our first view of Meiringen.

Lunch at the Hotel Sauvage (splendid).

Went in church where ten years ago I played the organ. Went through Gorge of the Aare (wonderful) then railway to Reichenbach Falls (very beautiful).

Friday

Very wet. Went in museum and ancient church, Protestant. Interesting recent excavations under church. Left after lunch, train to Brienz, steamer past Griesbach to Interlaken. Lovely tea at Lake Hotel (Seiler) and railway to Grindelwald. Wonderful scenery, could not see to advantage owing to mist. Hotel Schonegg <u>very excellent</u>.

Saturday

Glorious morning. Very early woke. Saw magnificent view from bedroom window, perfectly lovely. Early out enjoying the beautiful gardens of the hotel. Walked about the valley at various parts enjoying this delightful place. Oh, to stay here longer. Shops interesting, tea at charming café.

Sunday

Saw two climbers on the snow slopes of the Wetterhorn through telescope. Perfectly wonderful day again. Very hot, everything looking simply gorgeous. Service at English Church, large congregation, about 300 people. Left 2.16 for journey home. Beautiful views down the valley, saw the Jungfrau at Interlaken. Via Lake Thun, thence from Zweisimmen to Montreux via the wonderful mountain railway. Magnificent scenery for miles, wonderful sunset as we descended from Les Avants to Montreux. Glorious views of the Lake of Geneva. Stroll by the lake, had two hours to wait for our Paris train. Arrived Victoria, Monday 7pm.

18.

July 1932
Waterhead, Lake Windermere

Saturday

Moonlight trip round the islands.

Sunday

By boat to Wray Castle for service at Wray Church.

Figure 121: *Wray Castle*

The castle belongs to the National Trust and is used for hikers. Afternoon by lake, terrifically hot. Evening walked to Rydal Water by the Rydal, crossing the Pelter Bridge.

Monday

Walked up the Kirkstone pass, 3 miles. At Kirkstone Inn, height is 1500. Bus to Ullswater, passing Brothers Water. At Ullswater rested by lake, returning by bus. Tea at Kirkstone Inn, walking back to Ambleside by the pass.

Tuesday

Motor launch down Lake Windermere to Lakeside. Bus to Grange-over-Sands.

Wednesday

Figure 122: *Wordsworth's seat*

Footpath by the Rydal to Rydal Water and Loughrigg Terrace to Grasmere. In churchyard, Wordsworth's grave. Dove Cottage, Wordsworth's home in the village. At Rydal, Nab Cottage, Ruskin. Returned by main road, thus circling the lake. Crossed the Rothay at Rydal, returning along the lower path by its strand. Rydal Water, one of the smallest of the attractive lakes, on a low rock reached by steps is Wordsworth's seat. Grasmere, one of the prettiest lakes.

Thursday

To Hawkshead, very quaint house. Wordsworth's school, founded 1658, Wordsworth's cottage. A very small Wesleyan chapel, picturesquely built between two houses. To Esthwaite Water, walked to Lake Coniston. Lunch on Hawkshead Hill at the Post Office, a tiny cottage. Here is small Baptist Chapel, built between two cottages. Coniston Lake and village. Returned by bus. Tea at Dodd's, Ambleside, then a walk to the Stock Ghyll Force.

Evening, watched a delightful sunset. At 11pm, still light with the remains of the sunset.

Friday

To Dungeon Ghyll Force via Skelwith Bridge, Elterwater, Langdale. Here is the Langdale Valley, a great centre for climbing (HF Rock Climbing Centre). Circled Lingmoor, 3 miles, thus obtaining magnificent views of the Langdale Valley and Pikes. Passed the footpath which leads over the pass to Borrowdale and Blea Tarn. At Elterwater, took field path by the river, passing the lake to Skelwith Bridge and then to Waterhead. After dinner, by the lake.

Saturday

From Windermere via the Troutbeck Valley and Kirkstone Pass through Patterdale to Glenridding. Walked up 'Sticks Pass' road about a mile, crossed the common over to the Helvellyn Road.

Evening, climbed Keldas, a good viewpoint for Ullswater Lake (National Trust) and surroundings.

Sunday

Wesleyan Chapel. Afternoon, up the lake to Pooley Bridge. Stiff climb to top of Bower Bank, returned by the lakeside road.

Monday

Figure 123: *Howtown Pier*

Steamer to Howtown, then via the Martindale road for sandwich. We then climbed through Boredale, skirting Place Fell, 2154. At the top obtained a magnificent view: Kirkstone Pass, Brothers Water, Helvellyn 3116, Grisedale, Patterdale, Glenridding and the lake. 750 acres in this district are administered by the National Trust.

Tuesday

Left Ullswater by bus for Keswick, passing along the lakeside road to the Keswick road by Aira Force, Dockray and Matterdale to the Penrith Road. Booked for our last week at the Borrowdale Hotel, 3 miles from Keswick and situated on Lake Derwentwater and in the Borrowdale valley.

Fine views of the Skiddaw range (3063), Catbells and the lake are obtained from the hotel. The Derwent fells are on the other side of the lake and opposite our hotel. A large house by the side of the lake is the home of Hugh Walpole.

Wednesday

Through the Borrowdale valley, passing the village of Grange to Rosthwaite, a charming place set in a delightful valley. Taking the path over the fells to Watendlath, we obtained magnificent views of the valley, 847ft, said to be one of the best views of the lakes and fells. At the Tarn are a few houses. Here lived 'Judith Paris' (Hugh Walpole).

Returned by the Lodore Falls, which are disappointing in dry weather.

Thursday

Bus through the Borrowdale valley and following the River Derwent to Seatoller. At this point the road ends and the only way out of the valley is the rough track over the Honister Pass to Buttermere. The highest point is about 1200ft. We passed the Cumberland Granite Company, which has a huge quarry through the pass.

At Buttermere we passed the length of the lake to Crummock Water. At this point we joined the bus route for Cockermouth, Wordsworth's birthplace.

Thence via Embleton to the Bassenthwaite Lake and Keswick.

Friday

Wet morning. Crossed the footpath to other side of Derwentwater. Walked along Catbells to Portinscale of Keswick. Delightful views.

At Friars Crag there is a very fine view of Derwentwater 'the most beautiful of England's lakes'. On the top is erected a monument of Ruskin.

Tea at the hotel (Borrowdale) with the Misses Cornell and Pullen.

Saturday

Figure 124: *Calder Abbey*

Motor trip to Wastwater and Wasdale. From the Market Place, Keswick, by the left side of Bassenthwaite Lake and the foot of the Lodore Fells, with Skiddaw on our right. We obtained a magnificent view of the lake and Keswick and surrounding peaks. Via Lorton down to Loweswater and Crummock Water through Lamplugh, church and hall 1595, over moorland and past a stone circle on Caw Fell. In the distance could be seen the Irish Sea and the faint outline of the Isle of Man.

To Calder Abbey, founded 1134, Ponsonby Hall, 1798. After leaving the mountainous country at Lorton we came into it again at Wasdale. At Wasdale Head the scenery increases in grandeur, rugged and windswept. Great Gable overlooks The Sty, The Screes, Scafell 3210. Wastwater has the smallest church, the deepest lake and the highest mountain.

We walked up the Sty Pass road to the small church. The pass leads over to Seathwaite. Returning via the coast, skirting Seascale, St Bees,

Whitehaven to Cockermouth.

At Bassenthwaite Lake we came by Skiddaw Terrace into Keswick. Here, according to Southey, is obtained the best view of Derwentwater.

Sunday

Figure 125: *Crosthwaite Church*

To Crosthwaite Church; preacher the Bishop Taylor Smith, every available seat taken. Present fabric fourteenth century, although a church has stood on this spot before the eleventh century. Southey's grave is here and a memorial in the church.

Afternoon in the beautiful garden of the hotel with a fine view of the Derwent Fells. Before dinner we walked to Rosthwaite and climbed Castle Crag in endeavouring to cross it and reach Grange – hereby hangs a tale. For we never reached Grange, but retraced our steps and got the last bus by the skin of our teeth at Rosthwaite.

Monday

Walked by Derwentwater and Ashness Bridge. Took footpath to Friars Crag. Spent the morning looking at the shops in Keswick. Returned to Borrowdale for lunch, took an early tea in the garden. Bus to Seatoller.

Just short of Seatoller is the path leading to the Sty Pass and Sty Head to Wasdale. We took this path, following the Derwent, and walked nearly to Seathwaite, said to be the wettest inhabited place in England. We had sunshine and on the hills were to be seen several waterfalls.

Retracing our steps we returned via Rosthwaite – here is a path leading to the Stake Pass which leads to the Langdale Valley. After dinner climbed the hill at back of hotel, watched the men making hay in the valley and the stillness impressed us, only broken by the birds and life of the country.

Tuesday

From Keswick, bus for Windermere, passing Thirlmere – now a reservoir used by the Manchester Corp. To Grasmere and Rydal down to Ambleside and Windermere. Thus ended a delightful holiday spent amongst the hills and on the lakes, employing ridges and moorland tracks in this beautiful country with so many and varied places of interest. The foot alone can conquer the Lake Country.

Fourteen lakes, four main peaks over 3000, hundreds over 2000, small area 20 mile circle, Grasmere the centre.

19.

August, 1938
Switzerland

August 6. Dover – Ostend. Basle. Montreux, Dent du Midi Hotel

Figure 126: *Dent du Midi Hotel, Montreux*

August 7. Evening, Church.

August 8. Afternoon, via lake to Castle of Chillon.

August 9. Great St Bernard Pass and Gt. St Bernard Hospice. Italian frontier.

Figure 127: *Great St Bernard Hospice*

August 10. Day spent by lake.

August 11. Geneva via lake. Town, League of Nations.

August 12. Shopping. Afternoon, Glion, village above Montreux.

August 13. Train via Brig to Kandersteg. Hotel Baren, foot of Gemmi Pass.

August 14. English Church, morning service. Afternoon, Waldhaus Hotel. Good climb.

August 15. Village and walk up Gemmi Pass.

August 16. Oeschinensee, two-hour climb. Sat by lake two hours. Dance and concert, hotel.

Figure 128: *Oeschinensee*

August 17. Rail to Spiez, Lake Thun to Interlaken. Rail to Blue Sea.

August 18. Day at hotel.

August 19. Rail to Bern, Hotel Bellevue. Lunch. Basel three hours, Rialto evening.

August 20. Ostend, Dover 4pm. Chesham Bois 7pm.

Acknowledgements

Fig 1: Ramsay Lodge and Ramsay Garden. David Monniaux (https://commons.
wikimedia.org/wiki/File:Edinburgh_old_town_dsc06355.jpg), Edinburgh old
town dsc06355, https://creativecommons.org/licenses/by-sa/3.0/legalcode

Fig 2: John Knox House, Edinburgh. Kim Traynor (https://commons.wikimedia.org/
wiki/File:John_Knox's_House_-_geograph.org.uk_-_3060967.jpg), https://
creativecommons.org/licenses/by-sa/3.0/legalcode

Fig 3: Golden Lion Hotel, Stirling. Courtesy of Stirling Local History Society

Fig 4: Cauldron Linn. Iain McDonald (https://commons.wikimedia.org/wiki/
File:Waterfall_on_River_Devon_-_geograph.org.uk_-_37183.jpg), https://
creativecommons.org/licenses/by-sa/2.0/legalcode

Fig 5: Craigendoran Station. Reproduced by kind permission of Helensburgh Heritage
Trust

Fig 6: Craigendoran Pier. Reproduced by kind permission of Helensburgh Heritage
Trust

Fig 7: Trossachs Hotel. David Neale (https://commons.wikimedia.org/wiki/File:An_
Tigh_Mor_Holiday_apartments_-_geograph.org.uk_-_41310.jpg), https://
creativecommons.org/licenses/by-sa/2.0/legalcode

Fig 8: Falls of Tummel. Image Copyright Euan Nelson
This work is licensed under the Creative Commons Attribution-Share Alike 2.0
Generic Licence. To view a copy of this licence, visit http://creativecommons.
org/licenses/by-sa/2.0/ or send a letter to Creative Commons, 171 Second
Street, Suite 300, San Francisco, California, 94105, USA.

Fig 9: Dunkeld Cathedral. Alison Stamp (https://commons.wikimedia.org/wiki/
File:Dunkeld_Cathedral.jpg), https://creativecommons.org/licenses/by-sa/2.0/
legalcode

Fig 10: Newlyn Harbour from Peter's Cornwall Genealogy.
(http://freepages.genealogy.rootsweb.ancestry.com/ ~peterscornishfamily)

Fig 11: Penberth Cove, www.ronebergcairns.com

Fig 12: Logan Rock, Cornwall. Jim Champion (https://commons.wikimedia.org/wiki/File:Logan_Rock_from_below.jpg), https://creativecommons.org/licenses/by-sa/3.0/legalcode

Fig:13: Porthcurno School of Wireless Telegraphy. From http://telegraphmuseum.org, The Telegraph Museum, Portcurno.

Fig 14: Truro Cathedral. Simon Lewis (https://commons.wikimedia.org/wiki/File:Truro_stmarysst.jpg), https://creativecommons.org/licenses/by/2.5/legalcode

Fig 15: On the Way to Calvary by Tinworth. Photographer, Robin Banerjee from Victorianweb.com

Fig:16: Cahernane House Hotel. Reproduced by kind permission of the Cahernane House Hotel.

Fig 17: Killarney House. Free of copyright.

Fig 18: Gap of Dunloe. Free of copyright.

Fig 19: Colleen Bawn Caves. From *Ireland, Historic and Picturesque* by Charles Johnston. Not in copyright.

Fig 20: Muckross Abbey. Free of copyright.

Fig 21: Macgillicuddy's Reeks. Matpib (https://commons.wikimedia.org/wiki/File:MacGuillycuddy's_Reeks.jpg), https://creativecommons.org/licenses/by-sa/3.0/legalcode

Fig 22: Torc Cascade. Snapshots Of The Past (https://commons.wikimedia.org/wiki/File:Torc_Cascade._Killarney._Co._Kerry_Ireland.jpg), https://creativecommons.org/licenses/by-sa/2.0/legalcode

Fig 23: Glengariff Tunnels. Snapshots Of The Past (https://commons.wikimedia.org/wiki/File:Tunnel_Near_Glengariff._Co._Cork_Ireland.jpg), https://creativecommons.org/licenses/by-sa/2.0/legalcode

Fig 24: Bantry Fair. Digital copy courtesy of Cork City Libraries www.corkpastandpresent.ie. From *The South of Ireland* illustrated: with descriptive letterpress and maps. Cork: Guy & Co., 1904(?)

Fig 25: Cromwell's Bridge. No known restrictions on publication.

Fig 26: Jaunting Car. No known restrictions on publication.

Fig 27: Gimblet Rock. Alan Fryer (https://commons.wikimedia.org/wiki/File:Carreg_yr_Imbill_-_Gimblet_Rock_Pwllheli.jpg), https://creativecommons.org/licenses/by-sa/2.0/legalcode

Fig 28: Pwllheli Tram. By kind permission of John Prentice, Tramway and Light Railway Society

Fig 29: Glynn-y-Wyddw house. Image Copyright Penny Mayes. This work is licensed under the Creative Commons Attribution-Share Alike 2.0 Generic Licence. To view a copy of this licence, visit http://creativecommons.org/licenses/by-sa/2.0/ or send a letter to Creative Commons, 171 Second Street, Suite 300, San Francisco, California, 94105, USA

Fig 30: Miner's bridge. Courtesy of Judges Sampson Ltd, www.judgesampson.com.

Fig 31: Grand National Hotel, Lucerne. Free of copyright.

Fig 32: Rigi mountain railway. Kabelleger/David Gubler (http://www.bahnbilder.ch) (https://commons.wikimedia.org/wiki/File:VRB_H_1-2_bei_Freibergen.jpg), https://creativecommons.org/licenses/by-sa/3.0/legalcode

Fig 33: Pilatus Railway. Free of copyright.

Fig 34: Wiliam Tell's Chapel. Roland Zumbühl (https://commons.wikimedia.org/wiki/File:Tellskapelle2000.jpg), https://creativecommons.org/licenses/by-sa/3.0/legalcode

Fig 35: Kapellbrucke. Luzern Ikiwaner (https://commons.wikimedia.org/wiki/File:Luzern_Kapellbruecke.jpg), https://creativecommons.org/licenses/by-sa/3.0/legalcode

Fig 36: Lion monument, Luzern edwin.11 (https://commons.wikimedia.org/wiki/File:Lowendenkmal_(2521451200).jpg), https://creativecommons.org/licenses/by/2.0/legalcode

Fig 37: Hotel Sauvage, Meiringen. Reproduced from an old postcard, courtesy of Thomas Joss.

Fig 38: Gorge of the Aare. This image was taken by Craig Stanfill and is reproduced under Creative Commons licence 2.0.

Fig 39: Giessbach Falls and Hotel. From an old postcard, courtesy of Giessbach Foundation.

Fig 40: Kursaal, Interlaken. By kind permission of Kursaal, Interlaken.

Fig 41: Kleine Scheidegg. Free of copyright.

Fig 42: Baregg glacier. Free of copyright.

Fig 43: Lynton and Barnstaple railway. Reproduced from an old F. Frith & Co postcard.

Fig 44: Lynmouth, Mars Hill. Reproduced from an old F. Frith & Co postcard.

Fig 45: Lynmouth, Watersmeet and Cottage. Reproduced from an old F. Frith & Co postcard.

Fig 46: Foreland Lighthouse. Christopher Ware (https://commons.wikimedia.org/wiki/File:Foreland_Point_lighthouse_-_geograph.org.uk_-_457819.jpg), https://creativecommons.org/licenses/by-sa/2.0/legalcode

Fig 47: Clovelly High Street, looking down. Reproduced from an old F. Frith & Co postcard.

Fig 48: Hunter's Inn. Reproduced from an old postcard.

Fig 49: Badgworthy Valley. Reproduced from an old postcard.

Fig 50: Countisbury Hill. Reproduced from an old F. Frith & Co postcard.

Fig 51: Penrose almshouses, Barnstaple. Free of copyright.

Fig 52: Statue of Charles Kingsley, Bideford anonymous (https://commons.wikimedia.org/wiki/File:Charles_Kingsley_-_Bideford_(2006-03-04).jpg), https://creativecommons.org/licenses/by-sa/3.0/legalcode

Fig 53: Point-in-View church. By kind permission of the chaplain, Point-in-View.

Fig 54: The Boyhood of Raleigh. Free of copyright. https://commons.wikimedia.org/
wiki/File:Millais_Boyhood_of_Raleigh.jpg

Fig 55: Crossmount, St Columb Minor. By kind permission of Rev. Chris McQuillen-
Wright, Newquay Anglican Churches.

Fig 56: Watergate Bay and Hotel. Reproduced from an old F. Frith & Co postcard.

Fig 57: St Mawgan Church. Reproduced from an old F. Frith & Co postcard.

Fig 58: Porth Sands. Reproduced from an old F. Frith & Co postcard.

Fig 59: Huer's hut, Newquay. Reproduced from an old postcard by Judges Ltd,
Hastings.

Fig 60: Trerice House. Andrew Longton (https://commons.wikimedia.org/wiki/
File:Trerice1.jpg), https://creativecommons.org/licenses/by-sa/2.0/legalcode

Fig 61: Norwegian Rock. Image Copyright Derek Harper. This work is licensed under
the Creative Commons Attribution-Share Alike 2.0 Generic Licence. To view a
copy of this licence, visit http://creativecommons.org/licenses/by-sa/2.0/ or send
a letter to Creative Commons, 171 Second Street, Suite 300, San Francisco,
California, 94105, USA.

Fig 62: St Piran in the Sands. From www.stpiran.org, St Piran Trust.

Fig 63: Tintagel. Reproduced from an old F. Frith & Co postcard.

Fig 64: St Symphorian, Forrabury. By kind permission of https://www.iwalkcornwall.
co.uk

Fig 65: Banqueting Hall cave. Reproduced from an old postcard by Judges Ltd,
Hastings.

Fig 66: Maer Lake, Bude. Reproduced from an old postcard.

Fig 67: Tree Inn, Stratton. By kind permission of the Tree Inn.

Fig 68: Mill House, Combe. John of Reading (https://commons.wikimedia.org/wiki/
File:Coombe,_Bude_-_Mill_House.jpg), https://creativecommons.org/licenses/
by-sa/4.0/legalcode

Fig 69: Tonacombe Manor. Reproduced from an old postcard.

Fig 70: Rev. R S Hawker. Free of copyright.

Fig 71: Hawker's Hut. Humphrey Bolton (https://commons.wikimedia.org/wiki/
File:Hawker's_Hut,_Vicarage_Cliff,_Morwenstow_-_geograph.org.uk_-
_1369016.jpg), https://creativecommons.org/licenses/by-sa/2.0/legalcode

Fig 72: Old Poultry Cross, Salisbury. Courtesy of Salisbury Museum©.

Fig 73: Farrant Hayes, Branscombe. Reproduced from Google Streetview, Image
capture Sep. 2009 ©2016 Google.

Fig 74: Beer, Devon. Free of copyright.

Fig 75: Salcombe Regis. From www.oldukphotos.com

Fig 76: Sidmouth Esplanade. From www.oldukphotos.com

Fig 77: Royal Glen, Sidmouth. By kind permission of http://olddevonheritage.org

Fig 78: Ottery St Mary church. Image Copyright Richard Rogerson. This work is
licensed under the Creative Commons Attribution-Share Alike 2.0 Generic

Licence. To view a copy of this licence, visit http://creativecommons.org/licenses/by-sa/2.0/ or send a letter to Creative Commons, 171 Second Street, Suite 300, San Francisco, California, 94105, USA.

Fig 79: Barmouth Bridge. E Gammie (https://commons.wikimedia.org/wiki/File:Barmouth_bridge_-_geograph.org.uk_-_1315812.jpg), https://creativecommons.org/licenses/by-sa/2.0/legalcode

Fig 80: Coes Fan. Trevor Rickard (https://commons.wikimedia.org/wiki/File:Coesfaen_-_geograph.org.uk_-_462885.jpg), https://creativecommons.org/licenses/by-sa/2.0/legalcode

Fig 81: Orielton Hall. From www.oldukphotos.com

Fig 82: Cors-y-Gedol hall. With kind permission of Cors-y-Gedol Hall.

Fig 83: Lloyd George's house, Criccieth. From www.oldukphotos.com

Fig 84: Cregennan Lake. Image Copyright Martin Creek. This work is licensed under the Creative Commons Attribution-Share Alike 2.0 Generic Licence. To view a copy of this licence, visit http://creativecommons.org/licenses/by-sa/2.0/ or send a letter to Creative Commons, 171 Second Street, Suite 300, San Francisco, California, 94105, USA.

Fig 85: Foxes Path, Cader Idris. By kind permission of Dave and Angie Walsh.

Fig 86: Dunster, Somerset. Reproduced from an old J. Salmon postcard.

Fig 87: Grabhurst. Reproduced from an old postcard published by the Postcard Company, London and Tunbridge Wells

Fig 88: Dunkery Beacon. Martin Bodman (https://commons.wikimedia.org/wiki/File:Dunkery_Beacon.jpg), https://creativecommons.org/licenses/by-sa/2.0/legalcode

Fig 89: Old Ship Inn, Porlock. From www.oldukphotos.com

Fig 90: Cleeve Abbey. James Denham (https://commons.wikimedia.org/wiki/File:Cleevecloister.jpg), https://creativecommons.org/licenses/by-sa/2.0/legalcode

Fig 91: Cloutsham Farm. From www.oldukphotos.com

Fig 92: Selworthy Green. From www.oldukphotos.com

Fig 93: Dellers restaurant, Exeter. Free of copyright.

Fig 94: The approach to Princetown station. Reproduced from an old postcard out of copyright.

Fig 95: Two Bridges. Reproduced from an old postcard.

Fig 96: Sir James Brooke, Rajah of Sarawak. Free of copyright.

Fig 97: Bedford Hotel, Tavistock, 1920. By kind permission of the Bedford Hotel.

Fig 98: Clapper bridge, Dartmeet. Image Copyright Cathy Cox. This work is licensed under the Creative Commons Attribution-Share Alike 2.0 Generic Licence. To view a copy of this licence, visit http://creativecommons.org/licenses/by-sa/2.0/ or send a letter to Creative Commons, 171 Second Street, Suite 300, San Francisco, California, 94105, USA

Fig 99:   Plymouth Guildhall Square. From www.oldukphotos.com
Fig 100: Agnes Weston Home, Plymouth. By kind permission of Aggie Weston's.
Fig 101: Agnes Weston. By kind permission of Aggie Weston's.
Fig 102: Submarines, Falmouth. Free of copyright.
Fig 103: St Anthony's lighthouse. Free of copyright.
Fig 104: Portscatho Express. By kind permission of St Just and
St Mawes Heritage Group.
Fig 105: Nice Casino. Reproduced from an old postcard.
Fig 106: Russian Orthodox church, Cannes. Иерей Максим Массалитин
(https://commons.wikimedia.org/wiki/File:ACOR-Cannes.jpg), https://
creativecommons.org/licenses/by-sa/2.0/legalcode
Fig 107: Vence. Photo: Myrabella/Wikimedia Commons/CC BY-SA 3.0 (https://
commons.wikimedia.org/wiki/File:Vence.jpg), https://creativecommons.org/
licenses/by-sa/3.0/legalcode
Fig 108: Pont du Loup viaduct. Reproduced from an old postcard.
Fig 109: Garibaldi monument, Nice. Martin Putz (https://commons.wikimedia.org/wiki/
File:Nice_Place_Garibaldi_1.jpg), https://creativecommons.org/licenses/by-
sa/3.0/legalcode
Fig 110: Batavier III. Free of copyright.
Fig 111: Marken fisherman. Free of copyright.
Fig 112: Peace conference, 1899, The Hague. Free of copyright.
Fig 113: Hotel Bellevue, Dordrecht. Reproduced from an old postcard.
Fig 114: The Old Hall, Askrigg. By kind permission of https://www.thedales.org.uk
Fig 115: Aysgarth Falls. Wehha (https://commons.wikimedia.org/wiki/File:Aysgarth_
Lower_Force.JPG), https://creativecommons.org/licenses/by-sa/3.0/legalcode
Fig 116: English Church, Zermatt. Andrew Bossi (https://commons.wikimedia.org/wiki/
File:3696_-_Zermatt_-_Englischerkirche.JPG), https://creativecommons.org/
licenses/by-sa/2.5/legalcode
Fig 117: Gorner Gorge. Free of copyright.
Fig 118: Kulm Hotel, Gornergrat. Ximonic (Simo Räsänen) (https://commons.
wikimedia.org/wiki/File:Gornergrat_station,_Wallis,_Switzerland,_2012_
August.jpg), https://creativecommons.org/licenses/by-sa/4.0/legalcode
Fig 119: Rhone Glacier, Gletsch. Free of copyright.
Fig 120: View of Furka Pass from summit of Grimsel Pass. Cooper.ch 10:27, 27 October
2006 (UTC) (https://commons.wikimedia.org/wiki/File:Furkapass_westside.
jpg), https://creativecommons.org/licenses/by-sa/3.0/legalcode
Fig 121: Wray Castle. CellsDeDells (https://commons.wikimedia.org/wiki/File:Wray_
Castle,_Windermere.jpg), https://creativecommons.org/licenses/by-sa/3.0/
legalcode
Fig 122: Wordsworth's Seat. Reproduced from a stock publicity photograph for the
Furness Railway. Out of copyright.

Fig 123: Howtown Pier. Karl and Ali (https://commons.wikimedia.org/wiki/File:A_ steamer_docking_at_Howtown_pier_(geograph_4632321).jpg), https:// creativecommons.org/licenses/by-sa/2.0/legalcode

Fig 124: Calder Abbey. Free of copyright.

Fig 125: Crosthwaite Church. Image Copyright Peter Trimming. This work is licensed under the Creative Commons Attribution-Share Alike 2.0 Generic Licence. To view a copy of this licence, visit http://creativecommons.org/licenses/by-sa/2.0/ or send a letter to Creative Commons, 171 Second Street, Suite 300, San Francisco, California, 94105, USA.

Fig 126: Dent du Midi Hotel. Free of copyright.

Fig 127: Great St Bernard Hospice. Roland Zumbühl, Arlesheim (https://commons. wikimedia.org/wiki/File:Grand_St-Bernard.jpg), https://creativecommons.org/ licenses/by-sa/3.0/legalcode

Fig 128: Oeschinensee. Roland Zumbühl (Picswiss), Arlesheim (Commons: Picswiss project) (https://commons.wikimedia.org/wiki/File:Oeschinensee.jpg), https:// creativecommons.org/licenses/by-sa/3.0/legalcode